"After pastoring in California for over 40 years, my wife, Peggy, and I moved to St. Louis, Mo. There in the church, we attended we met Don and Barb Kassebaum with whom we became close friends. At that time Don had a great burden and vision to minister to the poor of Guatemala. We helped him send large containers of clothes and furniture to bless the poor of Guatemala. He also had the vision to reach the lost of Guatemala through ministering spiritually to the churches and their outreaches. I went with Don four times to minister to the churches and their pastors. He also conducted evangelistic services, and many were won to Christ. I also went to India three times when he had evangelistic crusades in which many came to Christ. He also had the vision to provide a facility in Guatemala to minister to the orphans. A beautiful facility has been built and 75 orphans are living there now.

"I have come to love and respect Don because he is a great Christian leader and missionary. He is a man of great faith and love; zeal and wisdom; boldness and humility; and integrity and prayer. He is also a successful businessman and has a dedicated family who runs the business he started. They are all serving God and supporting missionary endeavors. His book, *He Will Make a Way*, is an appropriate title of his life and ministry. He has seen God work many miracles to bring about great success and fruitfulness. This book will inspire and challenge you to seek and do God's will and to trust in Him in spite of difficult circumstances. God will truly make a way for you."

-**Bill Gorrell**,
Previous Pastor in Ventura, C.A.

More praise for **"He Will Make a Way"**...

"I have truly enjoyed being able to read again about the many adventures and life lessons God has shown my parents. I have learned many things through the years from them but the thing that has impacted me most (and brought back to me again when reading the book) was the way they have truly lived a life of Faith in God. As you read this book, I encourage you to learn to live a life of complete trust in God for every situation you face. These are just two ordinary people who have believed God to do the extraordinary in their lives."

-**Derrik Kassebaum**,
Director and V.P. of Sales for Cosmos Corp.

"I started reading this book and went on an exciting journey with Don and Barb into their life, their family and their God-ordained Mission. This book is a testament of love for God and His people: **"The sacrifice of love for the Kingdom of God."** I am truly blessed by the commitment of Don, Barb and their family to see the Gospel of the Kingdom of God reach and serve the less fortunate in our world. They have time and time again given the ultimate sacrifice of love to meet the natural and spiritual needs of so many.

"This book will challenge all who love the Lord and His church to give from their heart, soul, and body to the Great Commission, that commands us to Go into all the World, preach the Gospel of the Kingdom of God, make disciples of all nations. My wife Sylvia and I are so blessed to be friends with Don, Barb and their family for nearly 40 years. May God continue to bless and keep you strong."

-**Major Johnson**,
Lead Pastor of Bread of Life Christian Center,
Carson California

"We have been so grateful for our relationship with Don and Barb Kassebaum that started nearly 40 years ago. During this time, I have witnessed the increased blessing, protection and favor of Almighty God on their lives and upon those of their family.

"The amazing blessing this couple has so generously been to so many is not without cause. The principles I have seen have been a deep provocation and encouragement to me and to many others. They are:

- The strengthening of an increasing faith through the daily disciplines of prayer, worship and a life of regular fasting.
- The willingness to step out in obedience to the voice of God and to risk all for the Glory of God.
- Their constant faithfulness, perseverance, and hunger in the pursuit of the Kingdom of God.
- Their generous love for God and people, especially for the poor and disenfranchised.

"Don and Barbara's example as disciples of the Lord Jesus demonstrates how God can take and use anyone who simply offers their heart to Him for His sake and for His pleasure.

"I strongly commend the reading of this testimony to challenge and provoke you to "follow them as they have followed Christ."

-**Mike Stevens**, author of *God's Grand Purpose...and Your Part in It*, *God's Grand Romance...and Your response to It*, *God's Grand Return...and Your Preparation for It*, *God's Grand Kingdom...and Your Invitation to Reign with the Lord Jesus*, and *70 Golden Threads of Grace The Principles of War.*

"Some people believe that miracles are rare; we discovered that miracles are the normal way God lives in His people. We knew our task was only to believe." These statements from the end of Chapter 3 beautifully sum up the lives of Don and Barb Kassebaum and their journey together. Vulnerability and candidly (with a dash of humor thrown in), Don shares his stories of both their highs and lows in a manner that encourages the reader to believe God could actually use them also to advance His Kingdom. Repeatedly, the theme of prayer, obedience and watching for God to move is woven throughout each chapter. Don's testimonies of God at work left me wanting to hear even more!"

-**Tom Kyle**,
Senior Pastor of Life Church,
St. Peters Missouri

He Will Make a Way

He Will Make a Way

MIRACLES ARE THE NORMAL
WAY GOD LIVES IN HIS PEOPLE.

DONALD KASSEBAUM

XULON PRESS

Xulon Press
2301 Lucien Way #415
Maitland, FL 32751
407.339.4217
www.xulonpress.com

© 2018 by Donald Kassebaum

All rights reserved solely by the author. The author guarantees all contents are original and do not infringe upon the legal rights of any other person or work. No part of this book may be reproduced in any form without the permission of the author. The views expressed in this book are not necessarily those of the publisher.

Some names have been changed to be used in place of actual names.

Unless otherwise indicated, scripture quotations are taken from The New King James Version. Copyright © 1979, 1980, 1982 by Thomas Nelson, Inc.; The HOLY BIBLE, NEW INTERNATIONAL VERSION,. Copyright © 1973, 1978, 1984 by International Bible Society and The Holy Bible, King James Version. Copyright © 1972 by Thomas Nelson Inc., Camden, New Jersey 08103. Used by permission. All rights reserved.

Printed in the United States of America.

ISBN-13: 978-1-54564-891-9

Blessing
Don Kenebaw

Dedication

*I dedicate this book to Barb, my wife.
My best friend and the love of my life!*

ACKNOWLEDGMENTS

I am so appreciative and thankful to all those who have helped me and encouraged me along the way of writing this book. First, I want to thank Barb, my wife who has forever been with me in every need I faced in writing this book over the past three years. Without her diligence of helping me with punctuation, spelling, content, and encouragement by just being at my side, I would not be putting these words on paper today.

So now I begin by giving thanks to God for putting me in contact with all those who played a part in my life's story of showing God's faithfulness. I want to thank my friend and brother in the Lord, Bernie Rains. Bernie, a writer himself, stayed with me to critique the content and writing of this book. His corrective suggestions were amazing to me.

I give thanks to our Lord for putting me in contact with the staff at Xulon Press. They also have helped me put the manuscript together. I give a special thanks to Dr. Larry Keefauver and his staff for spending many hours bringing the stories of my life alive. He has taken my manuscript and added much interest to the writing and format of the book. Dr. Larry has been a prince of a man to work with.

I continue to thank God for the friendship of many brothers and sisters in Guatemala who frequently exhorted me to continue forward with the stories of my life. I especially want to thank Victor Sosa, my good friend and spiritual son in the Lord. He was the first person to encourage me, more than twenty years ago, to write a book about the incredible stories of salvation that God was taking my wife Barb and me through. Since then, many others have also given me the same encouragement.

I am thankful to Ray Hummel, who presently is home with Our Lord, for encouraging me to continue on writing. He told me countless times how he hoped to see the finished work. Today, though the book isn't published yet, Ray is worshipping and praising his Creator in heaven while the memories of his encouragements are always with me.

I want to acknowledge my four sons for releasing me from business matters while continuing to support my endeavors in writing this book. I especially give thanks to Denver for keeping my computer and all its functionality, working properly.

Mike Stevens, Bill Gorrell, Major Johnson, and Ben Settle have traveled with Barb and me to Guatemala and India teaching, preaching and administrating the flawless Word of God. Because of their efforts to respond to God's calling, we can write and tell of God's faithfulness to all of us who will receive.

Don and Barb Kassebaum Contact information:
E-mail address is dbkassebaum@mac.com.
www.giftsofloveintl.com

Contents

1 Planned Adventure.................................1
2 Tragedy and Triumph 27
3 Angels Follow Us 50
4 Perilous Encounters! 69
5 Prayer and Courage 84
6 Journeys of Enlightenment 101
7 Stressed but Blessed! 119
8 Time of Miracles! 141
9 Illegal in the Congo 157
10 Light in Dark Places............................171
11 A Change Is Coming...........................191
12 He Made a Gate Where There Was No Gate!.............207
13 Called to Preach 222
14 Help for the Abused............................236
15 Victors Not Victims.............................252
16 An Inescapable Crash 265

Chapter 1

PLANNED ADVENTURE

For there is a proper time and procedure for every delight...
(Ecclesiastes 8:6a NAS)

In the little town of Mattis, Missouri, I pedaled my bike as fast as my bony twelve-year-old legs would let me down the hill that was a notorious rite of passage for all young boys. I grinned as I passed my two older sisters, Midge and Barb. Halfway down the hill, my bike flipped, throwing me headfirst onto the pavement before crashing on top of me. My front wheel spokes caught my right foot and abruptly stopped my ride to glory. Midge continued riding passed me, but Barb stopped inquisitively. Seeing my bike was intact, she then checked to see if I was as lucky. After assuring Barb I was fine, she encouraged me to go home.

Arriving home my mom yelled, "Donald, (which normally meant trouble) I told you not to ride that bike so fast. Now put it away! You're grounded for the rest of the day."

Despite the punishment, I was glowing from the exciting mishap as an adventurous grin curled about my lips.

I was not a peculiar boy by any means—I liked speeding my bike down steep hills, had two loving parents, a large family, and behaved in school, at least as much as the other boys did. Even in my scrawny youth, I was levelheaded and had Midwestern resilience akin to the steady plains that surrounded me. I believed in luck and misfortune. I didn't question the circumstances of my world and had no reason to. My dreams were humble, and my path was straight.

As a small boy, I wanted to be a barber. Every time I needed a haircut, I went and sat and watched the barbers cut hair. I was captivated by their masterful performance and confident posture as they casually went about their work. The barber's hands seemed to circle about their canvas like a flock of birds, catching an updraft with fingers spread wide and then dive bombing back into the fray of unkempt hair. I was mesmerized.

Joining the Army

Our family had a strong Catholic heritage and mom wanted me to take the Sacrament of Holy Orders and join the clergy. However, Dad wanted me to follow in his footsteps as a machinist. When I was sixteen, mom enrolled me in a Catholic seminary summer program intended to get young boys interested in the priesthood. When I discovered that the only girls in the program were nuns, I decided to leave as soon as possible. With that calling clearly severed and the machinist's path uninteresting to me, at seventeen, I decided to join the Army after high school. Dad reluctantly took me to a recruiting station one evening to enlist for an eight-year commitment. I convinced my close friend Jim to sign up with me in the "buddy program." We would be trained for six months, then released to civilian life until the Army called us to active duty.

On July 18, 1960, the Army called, and we were assigned to Fort Leonard Wood, Missouri. When the day came for us to report, Jim had not yet received his induction papers, so I had to go alone. I was assigned a bunk and given instructions for the next day. Upon hearing the bugle call at 5 a.m., I was up and on my way to the mess hall. Eating quickly and returning to the barracks, I cleaned up my area and decided to rest for a few minutes. Waking up and finding no one else in the barracks, I took off running to the induction lines. As soon as I joined one of the long lines of inductees, I heard my name called "Kassebaum". Running to the front of the line launched an exciting day as I received vaccines, lost my hair, and was issued a uniform and boots. It wasn't until that evening, when admiring my smoothly shaved head in a handheld mirror, that I realized I was actually in the Army.

I lined up, marched, and shouted for eight weeks as I was quickly inducted into the rhythmic cadence of my newfound brotherhood. Those eight weeks of boot camp training broke down young recruits' individuality and built them up as a cohesive unit. After boot camp, I went through eight more weeks of training as a cook. I learned how to plan, prep, and cook a huge amount of food in the most efficient way possible. It might have seemed like a trivial task, but my job was not only paramount for my unit's success, it was also a daunting task to prepare meals for such a mass of hungry men.

I had not yet graduated from Cook School when I was assigned the task of cooking Thanksgiving dinner for about thirty-five soldiers and their families. I was the only cook with sixteen "KPs" (kitchen patrol), and only two of them even knew how to turn on a stove. Most of them could clean a rifle better than they could peel a potato. Miraculously, the meal went well. A week later, however, I saw soldiers passing out and stumbling to the ground after that night's dinner. Ambulances arrived to carry the sick to the infirmary and I later found out that food leftover from Thanksgiving dinner had become contaminated. I was spared blame because I was not that day's cook.

While still in Cook School, I became bed-ridden with pneumonia and was immediately put in the infirmary. My parents came to visit while I was fighting the infection. They brought with them a red and white 1957 Ford Fairlane 500 Skyliner with a convertible top. When I spotted the car, I was determined to leave the hospital.

Meeting the Girl of My Dreams

After recovering from pneumonia, I completed my training two days before Christmas and was released from duty for a while. On New Year's Eve, my friend Tony and I took our dates to a party. When I saw Tony's date, Barb, I thought she was the most beautiful girl I had ever seen. I quickly forgot about my own date and planned how to ask Barb out. Wasting no time, I made a date with her for the next weekend to go to the St. Louis Arena and watch "The Ice Capades."

Being with Barb was exhilarating. I was utterly enamored with everything about her. I got lost in her trusting eyes and charming smile.

The next morning at breakfast, I proudly announced, "Well, Dad, I know who is going to be my wife someday."

"Who's that?" Dad asked.

"She's the girl I met last night."

"Don't talk so silly," Dad said.

I knew what I wanted and drove my convertible to my aunt's house. She was an artist by trade and at my request, she painted *"Barbara Ann"* on the back, left side of my car. Now I was even prouder of my vehicle.

For the next four years, I served in a large battalion of soldiers stationed in St. Louis. We met every Monday night for 3 hours. Jim was assigned to my battalion's motor pool and one evening I talked Jim into surprising Barb. We took one of the monstrous M35 "Deuce and a Half" trucks ten miles off base to visit Barb. Jim reluctantly agreed but promised to kill me if we got caught. Lucky for me, we never did.

While fulfilling my army commitment, I worked as a stock clerk at a department store for nine months and waited to fulfill my dream of attending barber school. There was a year and a half waiting list to attend the school. Each week, I would contact the school in hopes of getting a positive response. Finally, in early November of 1961, I was told that there was an opening and I could start immediately. My response was quick, and I was in class the next day. In early spring of the following year, I graduated from "Moler's Barber College" and began my eighteen-month apprenticeship at a shop in Cedar Hill, Mo.

Marriage and Family

When I was nineteen years old, I married my sweetheart, Barb, and we became inseparable. Only thirteen months into our marriage, our first child was born. We named him, Donald Dale Jr.

Two months after our first baby was born, I finished my apprenticeship and opened my first barbershop in Sappington, Mo. The only customer on my first day was my dad, who insisted on paying the $1.50 charge for a haircut. I still have that first dollar. During the first week in my new adventure, I took in $35.00 and the second week $37.00.. The third week was the week before Christmas and I broke all records earning $95.00. As word spread around about my barbershop, I never earned less than $95.00 after that record week.

Barb, I and our new son lived in two rooms behind the barbershop until the landlord told us we had to move because the property was zoned commercial, not residential. It didn't take long before we found a duplex apartment for less than the weekly intake of the barbershop. It was more than spacious with three bedrooms, a living room, a kitchen, and two bathrooms.

Not too long after we signed the lease, the landlord asked us if we would be interested in buying the duplex. I doubted I had enough money or credit to buy the property but asked the selling price anyway. I was told the owner of the duplex had died and left it to his son who lived out of state. The son wanted $22,000 for the property. However, I told him the most I could offer was $11,000. The next day I received a call that the owner agreed to accept the $11,000. I was shocked, but quickly got a loan and purchased the property. We calculated that the rent from one apartment would make the loan payment and the second apartment rent could be used for a double payment. We were utterly dumbfounded by our good luck.

Before the joy of this fortune was gone, we received the good news that another baby was on the way. We named our new baby girl, Carol Ann. She was born fourteen months after Don Jr. Two years later, Barb's doctor told us another son was coming to join our family. Of course, this meant more diapers to change, crying to soothe, and babies to nurse, but we always dreamed that two boys and a girl would be the perfect size family.

We agreed, "We can handle this! This is good!" and named him Darin Daniel.

We decided to purchase three acres of land in a small community west of St. Louis and build a house that would be adequate for a family of five. A year later, another beautiful daughter was born. We named her Darlene Ann and she was the fourth great gift to our family. We were totally content with our beautiful family.

When we found out that another baby boy was on the way, we named him Derrik Drue and I thought, *Seven, that's a godly number. We'll raise five children. That shouldn't be too difficult for us. We can do it.* Just as we were getting settled with our five children, we found out we would be having another baby boy. He received the name Denver Dean and by this time, he was easy to care for. We were proud of our six beautiful children and knew that this was as large as our family should be.

Christian Clients

Amidst all the excitement of building a home and seeing our family grow, the barbershop in Sappington thrived and built a loyal clientele. Older men enjoyed sitting around talking as they received a haircut and the shop grew into a community space. More importantly, it was providing an adequate income for our family of eight. As more and more people started patronizing my shop, quite a few Christians were added as clients. No matter what everyone was talking about, these clients always seemed to end up talking about their religion. I had problems with some of what these Christians would say. For example, what they called the "born-again" experience, I thought was rather cultish.

Most assuredly, I say to you, unless one is born again, he cannot see the kingdom of God. (John 3:3)

I didn't want to cause any trouble or risk losing a client, so I just let it go. Sometimes I'd think, *I'm a Catholic, doesn't that automatically make me a Christian?* As these clients became more comfortable in my shop, they began saying things that seemed to challenge and even oppose my Catholic beliefs. Rather than let it cause any issues, I just focused on ways to improve my business and the barbershop.

As I kept an ear open to anything that might improve my trade and help my business, a client soon told me about a revolutionary method of cutting hair. After running it by another barber-friend, Hank, I agreed it was something worth looking in to. Barb also agreed I should pursue the program called Roffler Hair Styling. Although it required a pricey initial investment, the payoff would be worth it. The package came with training and a product line that produced professional results. I started my new Roffler Styling career and noticed a new strip mall was being built in the small town of High Ridge, Missouri, where we lived. We swiftly signed a lease and sold our barbershop in Sappington. I wasted no time in establishing a modern Roffler Men's Hair Styling Salon in the small country town. Some of the locals laughed at my styling salon for its fancy, modern look, but I welcomed the free advertisement. I did more business in those first five days than I ever did in a single week during the ten years I owned the shop in Sappington. We sat speechless as we counted our weekly tally.

A customer from Sappington named Ray, and his two sons, continued to come to me for their haircuts. Ray talked at length about the meeting place, named "The Sheep Shed," where his family went every Sunday morning and he invited me and my family to join them for breakfast along with a visit to the Sheep Shed.

I asked Ray if the place was a church, but Ray told me, "No, it's just a place where each Sunday morning a lot of people come and sing and somebody speaks about God."

As I considered Ray's invitation, I consulted with several clients who were Catholic priests. Every priest felt it would be wrong to take my family there, but I wasn't content with their dismissal. As I continued to weigh the issue, a new customer, who was also a priest, walked into my shop for a cut.

I asked him the same question and to my surprise, the priest answered in a confident tone, "Of course it would be fine. I have been invited and attended other denominational meetings myself. It all seemed fine to me. You must do as your conscience leads you."

That was exactly the answer I was waiting to capitalize on and that Sunday I brought the whole family to the Sheep Shed.

Meanwhile, a flood of Christian customers seemed to be patronizing my shop, all talking about Christianity and the teachings of Jesus. Many of the conversations centered around baptism. I even received letters concerning the matter from people I had never met. A customer named Mel would come in for a haircut every few weeks and talk to me about what it meant to be a Christian. I looked forward to Mel's visit and one evening when Mel was the last customer of the day, we talked for over two hours about receiving Jesus Christ as Lord and Savior. I had been sprinkled for water baptism as an infant, but Mel spoke about baptism by immersion.

When I left the shop late that evening, I went straight home to share what I had learned with Barb. While we were discussing the matter intensely on the couch, the inside of the house seemed to light up and our hearts felt eased and filled with happiness. It was as though a great burden had been lifted and we felt truly at peace. The Holy Spirit came upon both of us.

I was ready to be baptized by immersion. I had prayed about it for over a year, but I would never agree to it because of my love for the Catholic Church. I didn't want to leave what I knew. Once I agreed to baptism by immersion, I knew I was rejecting all allegiance to the Catholic Church. The pastor of The Sheep Shed, known as, New Covenant Church invited our whole family to come to a meeting on a Sunday evening when Dale Evans, the wife of Roy Rogers, gave her testimony of how she was given the name, "The Woman at The Well."

We sat in the back row of the church and I prayed if Dale gave an invitation for people to be baptized, I would go forward. Sure enough, she did just that. As Dale spoke the invitation, I leaned over and told Barb what was in my heart. Then I told the children I was going forward and any family member who wanted to go with me was welcome. Barb and our two eldest children went forward and stood at the platform with me. Then came our next eldest son. The five of us were baptized that night as God filled the longing in our hearts. It was a rush of emotion and thanksgiving. The baptism capped what was altogether a very foreign experience to the Catholic mass we were used to. The next day at work, the salon took on a new atmosphere. My clients took note of it, too. It looked lighter and more spacious than before.

During all of this, the Roffler training process helped me become a more skillful stylist. I even competed in men's hairstyling competitions where I regularly placed in the top three. Two years in a row, I won Missouri's first place hairstyling competition and was sent with three other award-winning hairstylists to national competitions at various locations around the country.

Bodily exercise profits a little, but godliness is profitable for all things, having promise of the life that now is and of that which is to come. (1 Timothy 4:8)

During a state wide competition, one of the judges happened to be a man I felt uneasy with and it was obvious that this judge didn't care for me. The competition involved giving two haircuts, the first was a "sculpture" cut, showing the accuracy of haircutting, and the second a "fashion" cut, producing the style and fashion of the day. I did my best but didn't feel there was any way to win first place, especially because of the unfriendly judge. I prayed diligently for God's favor and peace.

Each stylist had a number, my number was twelve. At the award's night, my whole family was there to cheer me on. I sat at a table in the back of the hall hoping that I would win either third or fourth place. I didn't feel there was any chance for second or first. When I heard someone else's number called for fourth place, I felt terrible. When my number wasn't called for third place, I wanted to just get up and leave. At that moment, I leaned over and put my head between my knees and heard another number called for second place.

My mind was screaming, "Why, Lord?" Then the last number was called; it was the number "12." I didn't hear it and stayed there with my head between my knees saying, "Why Lord?"

Then Barb started tapping me on the shoulder saying, "Don, Don, it's number 12. That's you, Don."

I lifted my head and heard my number called again. Upon hearing my number for first place, I raised my hands and arms to the Lord while running up to the front to receive my reward. I won a trophy for first place "sculpture cut" and a trophy for second place "fashion cut." I also received a medal on a ribbon for the first-place stylist of the year award. It was my night! I was learning to trust God even in the midst of my own doubts.

> *Trust in the LORD with all your heart and lean not on your own understanding.* (Proverbs 3:5)

God's Calling

Spring and summer meant camping and trout fishing for our family. From June through August the family would go on outdoor outings every month. Our favorite fishing hole was Montauk in southwestern Missouri. A highlight of the outdoor weekend was attending one of the church services in the area. One Sunday morning, at Montauk Baptist Church, a young couple was invited up front to be prayed over by the church leaders. As each leader took the microphone and began to pray for this couple, the words seemed to be directed at me. It was as if God was speaking directly to me through the words of these leaders.

I heard them say, "You are being set aside for My calling."

I was in denial as I thought, "No, this can't be. I love my work and my profession. This isn't from God. I won't receive it."

I loved cutting hair and my business was doing so well. Furthermore, cutting hair was how I started attending church. As I led my family out of the church, I was on edge and still refusing to accept what I heard.

As time passed and the jarring encounter at Montauk Baptist Church faded into daily life, I began to recognize God's calling and earnestly began to desire it. I prayed daily that God would open a door for me to have a job that didn't require physical work to earn a living for my family. Following this shift in perspective, a loyal client of the barbershop asked me if I would be interested in purchasing a beauty supply company. The company sold hairspray, shampoo, cosmetics, and other beauty products.

Through prayer, I became interested in this opportunity. However, the purchase price exceeded several hundred thousand dollars and seemed way out of my reach. Nonetheless, I couldn't shake my desire for this new opportunity. As I would go about my routine of talking to clients and cutting their hair, my mind drifted to the tempting possibilities that came with buying out the beauty supply company. Finally, I sat down to make a deal with the owner. The deal quickly formed as we agreed our duplex would become a small down payment and the owner would hold the note for an acceptable interest rate. The owner and I walked out smiling as it appeared the agreement was falling into place.

Then Barb and I met with their attorney and were presented with a new challenge—the seller was backing out of the agreement. Distraught and upset, I cried out to the Lord to make this sale come to pass. The very next day the owner called and again agreed to the sale. On October 31, we met with the sellers and attorneys to sign the paperwork for the purchase of the beauty supply company. By the end of the day, Barb and I owned both the barbershop and the beauty supply company. However, our celebration soon turned to panic as we discovered we did not own the inventory. It was another massive debt to acquire. We had never been in this much financial trouble. We learned quickly to draw on God's grace.

My grace is sufficient for you, for My strength is made perfect in weakness. (2 Corinthians 12:9)

In addition to the financial woes, I discovered some business practices in the company that created ethical problems for me. I had to make some serious changes. Consequently, that put pressure on the sales staff of seven. I promptly terminated two part-time salesmen and took over their territories. I also placed Don Jr. in as the bookkeeper. Along with all the personnel changes, I discovered that there was no inventory control in the warehouse and I needed to institute controls immediately. The remaining five salesmen became angry over these new policies that were cutting into their income. Through prayer and by faith, I decided to give all the sales staff an increase in salary. I knew that an unhappy sales staff could cause more trouble and the company was already in financial distress.

It wasn't long before I was feeling better about the staff. I believed they were all good men and I wanted to bless them. Then one of the salesmen didn't show up for work one Monday morning and later in the day sent notice that he had quit. I decided to take on that territory in addition to the other two territories I already worked. Although this created more work for me, the quitter's salary freed up some needed cash flow.

As a barber/hairstylist, I never needed to travel for my work. As a salesman, I found I was away from home every other week. While driving for long stretches in between sales calls, I was memorizing scriptures or singing worship music. This routine became energizing and I took naturally to selling. Even though I was the owner, I was always striving to be the top salesperson in the company.

Even though I was working hard, and the company was making strides, the bank called frequently to inform us there wasn't enough money in the account to clear all the checks that were trying to pass through. The pressure was mounting on the family because there was little money for food and not enough to pay the daily bills. When the bank called for money, we were given until 2 p.m. to get enough to clear the checks. When there wasn't enough money to clear all the checks, we used our home, which was free of debt, as collateral and the checks would then clear.

At one point, there was no more money to be drawn against the house because it was mortgaged to the limit. It was depressing given we owned the house outright when we purchased the beauty supply company. Through God's kindness, we found favor with the president of the bank and he helped us in so many ways. Also, the faithfulness of Don Jr. was immeasurable. He never asked for overtime pay even though he worked extra and always did his best to get all the bills paid. The company persisted in this chaotic cycle of financial difficulty for seven years without bankruptcy. It was nothing short of a miracle.

My God shall supply all your need according to His riches in glory by Christ Jesus. (Philippians 4:19)

As financial problems continued to mount, our whole family sought refuge with God in daily prayer. There was never a week that the bank didn't call for money, but somehow we were always able to pay our bills. One of the sacrifices we made for our survival was I never received a salary for seven years.

One particularly trying time, I was servicing a client in a town about four hours from home when the office called telling me the bank needed $5,000 to clear some checks. My heart sank as I remembered that there was no more collateral left in our house. I told Don Jr. to give me about forty-five minutes and I would give him an answer on what to do. While I was driving to the next town, I cried out to the Lord with all my heart for an answer.

God spoke to me and said, "This will be the last time you will borrow money."

I was elated. I didn't know what was going to happen, but I knew God had spoken. I called my son and told him what God had said. We both rejoiced on the phone. However, within a few days, the bank called again needing more money. I couldn't understand why because I knew I had heard from God.

I called my pastor again, who asked me, "What did the Man above say?"

Then I realized what God had said, "This will be the last time you will borrow money."

He didn't say that I wouldn't have the need again. So, I decided to just tell the bank the truth: we had no more money and to do whatever was necessary. We knew it was God's favor that sustained us when the checks would somehow get paid. We never knew how or by whom, but we didn't question the miracles happening for us.

Our Apache Camper

At church one Sunday there was an announcement for an expansion project offering to be taken at the next Sunday service. We had no money to give and sought God for guidance as to our giving. On Sunday morning, we still had no answer. As I met with a group of brothers before the service for prayer, God told me to donate our Apache camper. I genuinely wept as I remembered the many good times we had with it at our family outings. But God was adamant that this was His command. When Barb arrived at the church, I told her what God had spoken and she completely agreed. When the special offering was taken, I put a note in the basket to donate the camper.

He who sows sparingly will also reap sparingly, and he who sows bountifully will also reap bountifully. (2 Corinthians 9:6)

During the following week, no one responded to a local newspaper ad about the camper. I was relieved.

One day, a trucker saw the camper parked in the supply company's driveway and came into the building to inquire who owned it. I said, "I do".

"Do you want to sell it?" the trucker asked.

"Well, sure!" I said.

"How much?"

"How about $1,900?"

The trucker opened his wallet and gave me nineteen, $100 bills. I couldn't believe it.

"I'll be here Saturday to pick it up," said the trucker as he left.

Don Jr. and Darin Find Their Niche

After seven years of selling beauty supplies, Don Jr. and Darin wanted to introduce our own shampoo products to the pet industry. I was utterly opposed to being involved in the idea, feeling tired from the weariness of running a business. The boys were persistent and kept pressing to go to Naperville, Illinois, for a pet-grooming exhibition. I finally gave in and we traveled about five hours north to Naperville. We set up a small booth to display our products at the weekend exhibition. To our surprise, we gained more clients in those two days than our five salesmen were doing in one month. Traveling home from Naperville on Sunday night, we rejoiced in the Lord. The boys had found their niche and they placed their full effort towards launching into the pet industry.

A Winter Miracle

In mid-winter, Barb and I drove to California from High Ridge, Mo. to attend a beauty-supply convention. After three busy days at the conference, we journeyed home. About three a.m., I was awakened by Barb screaming. She was driving on ice coming through Oklahoma when I realized the car was spinning out of control on an ice-covered highway. Grabbing the steering wheel, I tried to gain control, but the car headed down an embankment and came to a sudden stop in deep snow.

As the silence settled, I heard a quiet, peaceful voice say, "Just pray."

Instead of praying, I tried to push open the driver's door. It would only open a few inches against the deep snow. I shifted the car in reverse, but when the rear wheels began to spin, the back of the car began to slide farther down the hill. As I applied the brakes, I remembered the words, "Just Pray."

"Let's pray," I said to Barb.

We prayed for a couple of minutes and then I put the car in reverse and with a little acceleration, backed up the hill through the deep snow and onto the icy highway. It appeared as though angels were pushing our car out of the snow. Back on the highway I drove ever so slowly on the icy pavement on our way to St. Louis.

Our trip to England

Late spring of 1982, Barb and I received an invitation to go to a Bible week in Wales, England. God provided all the resources for us to go from donors in the United States and England. I brought my barber tools with me to bless others. We stayed with a young couple in northern England. We shared stories of the many trials in the business we had back home and how we lived day-by-day trusting God. Our host told us about his friends who experienced very similar difficulties and how God brought them through. Upon leaving, I was given an envelope from our host asking me to read it on our train ride back to London. When the train pulled away from the station, I opened the letter in which he wrote they would be praying for us and our business. He wrote they knew God had sent us to them. He also put ten, £10.00 notes amounting to $175.00 in the envelope asking us to have a wonderful English breakfast before leaving for the States.

While traveling to London, I prayed with Barb about how to use this money to bless the Lord and His people. We thought that an early morning breakfast for our fellow U.S. travelers would be a great way to share God's blessing. While eating around a long table with thirty U.S. travelers, Keri, a good friend to all, came into the restaurant to thank each one individually for coming to England. Keri came to me last and asked me to step outside for a moment. As we went out the door of the restaurant, Keri asked me to put my hand out and he counted off twenty £5.00 notes equaling $175.00. Barb and I rejoiced in all that God had done. The timely gifts were confirmation that God was with us and continuing to take care of us.

Give, and it will be given to you. A good measure, pressed down, shaken together and running over, will be poured into your lap. (Luke 6:38)

Closing One Business and Growing Another

Back at home, Don Jr. announced he was engaged to be married. On October 8, 1983, he married his beautiful bride, Beth. She supported him in all his endeavors to make their marriage and the business grow. At the same time, this joyful wedding was being planned, the beauty supply business was failing and putting immense pressure on us. At different times some of the salesmen would come in on Mondays, turn in their sales for the previous week and complain about their jobs.

One Monday afternoon after a sales meeting closed and all the salesmen had left, I went outside and cried out, "Lord, I need Your help! I can't do this on my own anymore. Help me to know what to do."

Don Jr. heard me and came outside to find out what was wrong. I told him I just wanted out and to close the doors of the company.

He agreed and said, "Let's do it."

With that, we got in the car and went to our attorney's office to find out how to close the business. The attorney gave us advice and Barb and I agreed to pray and fast until God showed us the time to close the doors of the beauty supply company permanently. We prayed for our entire sales staff to find better jobs elsewhere and for God to soften their hearts to be able to receive the difficult news. We also prayed to erase the deficit.

For the next eight months, we prayed and fasted for three days each week as the business continued to struggle. After a weary season of seeking God's help, He answered us. When we went from a $42,000 deficit to a plus of $19,000, we knew it was time to go to each salesman and share with them the news we were closing the business. We found their hearts softened and their attitude sympathetic. As it turned out, each salesperson found a better job than they had at our company.

Paralleling the closure of the beauty supply company, the distribution of pet shampoo was growing rapidly. Our calendars were filled with pet grooming shows after the Naperville success. We began driving two weeks each month to pet shows from St. Louis to the east coast. We slept in the car when we couldn't afford hotels. Our goal was to gain ten new clients each week.

During the next year and a half, the company started to sustain the cost of a hotel room for whoever was on the road selling. As our business grew in the pet industry, we moved out of the beauty industry. God continued to answer our calls for help and showered us with a bountiful harvest in this exciting time of change. It seemed as though the years of hard and faithful labor were being rewarded.

The Lord is far from the wicked, but He hears the prayer of the righteous. (Proverbs 15:29)

"Don's army photo. Joining the army"

"Don's red and white Ford convertible brought to the army base by his mom and dad."

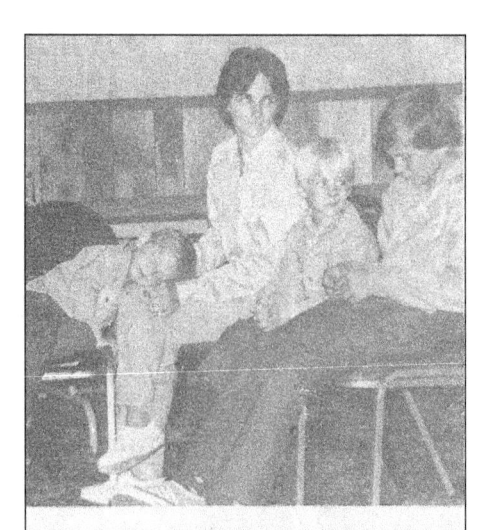

Styling is for the whole family, but the longer hours at the hairstyling sessions proved to be too much for some.

"Don's family waiting for results of Don's State of Missouri competition."

Planned Adventure

"Don displaying his trophies won in competition."

Hairstylists Prepare For Competition

THE MISSOURI STATE HAIR STYLING TEAM, made up of hairstyling competion winners from all over the state, pose outside team member Don Kessebaum's salon, where they are currently practicing for the national styling competition, to be held in Chicago in late September. Pictured are: Trainer Don Harbaugh, Louis Carson, Wil Stiles; Cliff Stotler, Don Kessebaum, and Trainer E.J. Pashia. (Staff photo).

"Don posing with hairstyling team."

"Family campout in Apache camper"

Chapter 2

TRAGEDY AND TRIUMPH

Am I now trying to win the approval of men, or of God? Or am I trying to please men? If I were still trying to please men, I would not be a servant of Christ. (Galatians 1:10 NIV)

My daughter, Darlene and I were invited by a friend, Geoff, to be part of a "Forward Edge" mission team going to Guatemala. Our assignment was to put a roof on a building that was to house 150 orphans. Excitement grew as we prepared to leave the states for ten days. On the plane, I told God I was going to serve in this project, but not get involved in any other long-term work in Guatemala.

When the plane landed, an elder from the church welcomed the team. We were shuttled for forty minutes to the construction site. It was an eye-opener for us on how another culture lives. Every little store on the way had window and door security bars over them and the houses were surrounded with block walls topped with razor wire. The team was given two gutted mobile homes to sleep in. The next day, after an uneasy night's rest, the construction work began.

There was plenty of help for the construction of the roof, so I volunteered to put new shock absorbers on an old van that was used for transporting children. I had no tools except a pair of pliers, a hammer, and a small socket set.

I spoke with the leader of the team about the condition of the tools and was told, "That's it. There are no others."

I thought, *Well Jesus, it's You and me.* It was a mechanical miracle. With God's help, I changed those shocks within three hours. During the remainder of the week, I cut children's hair at the orphanage and gave bows to the girls.

Each day I rose at 5:00 a.m. and prayed while walking along the construction site. I read God's Word at different intervals until the team members began to rise. One morning while reading, God spoke, "You are to return home and bring your family to Guatemala driving through Mexico. I will direct your steps." I began to weep believing these words came from the God of the universe. I promised God obedience to this call if my family, pastor, and home group leader were all in agreement.

When the construction of the roof was completed, a celebration gathering was held on Saturday night prior to the team's departure the next day. The team had a 7:15 a.m. flight back to the states and all went well.

The first evening back home around the dinner table, Darlene and I shared the events of our mission trip. I also spoke about my encounter with the Lord and how I had been directed to bring the family to Guatemala, driving through Mexico. I asked the family how they felt about going on a mission trip that summer.

Smiles appeared as Barb asked, "When will we go?"

"Just as soon as school ends," I said.

The three youngest children, with big smiles on their faces, were ready for a new adventure.

"Okay," I said. "I'll talk to our pastors Mike and Geoff this week. If they agree, we'll be on our way by early summer."

The next morning, I left on a business trip for Cape Girardeau, Missouri. The pet business was doing well. It was paying the bills and giving our families an adequate income. While driving on Interstate 55 south, I began thinking about my time in Guatemala. I remembered how I felt so close to God there. I knew Jesus as Savior, but now I wanted Him as my Lord. Shouting and crying out to the Lord, I could hardly see the highway, so I pulled onto the shoulder and wept. I wanted to serve the Lord with all my heart. I was ready to follow Jesus wherever He would lead. After a few minutes, I was back on the highway with blurry eyes, remembering God's command in Matthew 28:19.

Go and make disciples of all nations, baptizing them. . ..,and teaching them to obey everything I have commanded you. (Matthew 28:19)

Family Mission Trip to Guatemala

In early June, Barb and I took our two sons, our daughter, and her girlfriend Julie to Guatemala. It was a twenty-four-hour drive to the Mexican border from St. Louis. We had no problem crossing the border into Mexico, or so we thought. I drove about a mile from the border into Mexico when a young man waved his hands for us to stop. Barb rolled down her window and asked him what he needed. He asked us if we had stopped at the border to legalize the vehicle and ourselves in Mexico.

When we told him no, the man offered his help. We returned to the border with the young man who helped us through the entering and registering process. An hour later, he led us back to the highway going south. We financially blessed the man and thanked God for sending him. Darlene and her friend, Julie, could speak and understand some Spanish. Barb and I became dependent on them for directions.

I drove too fast and almost caused an accident with a big dump truck on a straight stretch of rough highway. We could barely see the vehicle a long distance ahead due to the dust flying all around us. Suddenly, I realized there was a dump truck unloading hot asphalt and there were about twelve men working on the side of the highway. I hit the brakes, but not soon enough. The workers took off running as the van began sliding, making deep ruts through the hot asphalt. Coming to a stop, I backed out of the deep ruts. The workers came running towards our vehicle with shovels waving. I wasted no time in leaving the scene of what could have had terrible consequences for everyone. I drove with much more caution after that incident.

I drove about two hundred and fifty miles south of the border, arriving in Tampico, Mexico at 2:00 p.m. I found a decent hotel and acquired three rooms. The next morning by 5:00 a.m., we were headed south on the highway. We saw a bakery and stopped to purchase some doughnuts. Upon entering the little store, we saw every ant of God's whole creation on the floor, walls, and counters of that building. We decided we weren't hungry after all.

By the end of the day, we came to the Port City of Vera Cruz. Driving along the coast, we saw a beautiful hotel and acquired three rooms. When we went to get our luggage from the van, we discovered we could not move the van. The President of Mexico had arrived and was staying at the same hotel. The streets were barricaded and there were soldiers and sailors dominating the entrances and exits to the hotel. We were now in the most secure place in all of Mexico for the remainder of the night.

After an early breakfast, we continued driving south and then west adjacent to Mexico's southern boundaries. At a crossroad, the map hinted to the right, but the directions from Sanborn's Travel Guide, we received at the border, directed us to go left. Unanimously, we decided to go to the left. Up into the mountains, we drove. The scenery was spectacular. There were whole tribes of Indians dressed in pink, white, and flowered clothing. Photos were not permitted. Men would get in front of the women blocking any photos.

We rested that night at a hotel in Tuxtla Gutiérrez and headed south again by 5:00 a.m. I got lost and ended up on a highway that turned into a dirt road after about two hours. I kept driving south until it turned back into asphalt, which led to the Guatemala border.

Upon arriving at the border we began the process of leaving Mexico. It took less than an hour and we were on our way into Guatemala. About fifteen miles south was the border town of, Tecum Umán. About thirty children ran out to the van wanting the job of helping us with the custom and immigration officials. We chose one of the boys to escort us to each office where I paid $5.00 to get the paperwork stamped and signed by each official. Finally, a gate was lifted and we officially entered Guatemala. Upon asking for directions to the Capitol City, we were told to follow the little white line on the highway. What a joke! The white line only lasted for about a mile and then we were lost again. Each time we saw someone who looked responsible, Darlene or Julie would ask for directions.

We arrived in Guatemala City late afternoon at the home of our friends, Ronny and Susie Gilmore. Ronny rented a home for us next to theirs. Shortly after arriving, an earthquake shook the house for more than seven seconds and frightened everyone. Was this a surprise welcome from heaven?

The next day, we went to the orphanage to inquire how we could serve. Barb was given a job of cleaning windows and I built closets. Our two sons, daughter, and Julie were given small jobs to do during their two-week mission project. Every Friday, Barb and I would take fifteen orphans to McDonalds. One Friday, all boys would go and the following Friday, the girls. I purchased a rose for each little girl when it was their turn. We were blessed when a missionary family decided to travel to the states with us when we left at the end of July.

During our time in Guatemala, God spoke a word of direction to Barb and me, "Go home and serve your elders there as you served the elders here in Guatemala. You will go and come and go and come." I realized that whatever the Guatemalan elders asked me to do, I did with joy in my heart. Now I was to return to my home and keep the same cooperative attitude with all elders.

Whatever you do, work at it with all your heart, as working for the Lord, not for men. (Colossians 3:23 NIV)

Traveling for four days on the highways of Guatemala, Mexico, and the U.S. we arrived home excited. The business was growing, and Don Jr. had done a great job running it on his own while we were gone. He told me that one day he would like to take over the business.

"It's time to take Cosmos, (the pet supply company) to a new level," he said as our new innovative shampoo system brought sudden growth to the pet industry. Don Jr., Darin, and I, with our new idea saved a groomer more than 30 percent of the monthly cost of shampoo. Time and frustration were also reduced in product application. When groomers heard there was no cost to purchase the system, but only a small monthly service charge, they were eager to try it.

We wasted no time building new business. I started meeting new clients in Georgia on Monday and Tuesday, then on to Miami on Wednesday. Leaving Georgia late, I tried to drive all night to be at my first salon by 8:00 a.m. Around 2:00 a.m. the fog was thick, and I was dozing at the wheel. I didn't want to stop. The next thing I knew I was in a bad storm, or so I thought. So much water was hitting the windshield that the wipers couldn't keep it clean. Then the engine stopped. Suddenly, I realized I had dozed off and ended up in a swamp. Upon opening the door, water was everywhere.

I jumped out of the van and climbed up an embankment. I got to a highway emergency phone to call for a tow truck. When the truck arrived, the driver worked quick and hard to get the van out of the swamp.

"If the police arrive," he said, "there could be problems."

Raising the hood on the engine compartment, I wiped the electronics dry, and by God's grace, when I turned the ignition key it started. A policeman drove up to see what had happened. I told him of the thick fog and how I couldn't see a hand in front of me. The policeman appeared so kind. I repented for not using a hotel that night and promised God that would not happen again.

Darin's Miracle

I had just returned from Florida when we received a call from Darin's doctor saying Darin was diagnosed with Hodgkin's disease. He was twenty-three years old at the time and had been having severe backaches plus there was a growth below his stomach. When the diagnosis of Hodgkin's disease was confirmed, the doctors recommended twelve months of Chemotherapy. The doctor told us Darin would need to complete all the treatments because if we stopped them he would never be able to start them again.

Darin began his treatments immediately. They were very difficult for him. I would drive him to the doctors office once every three weeks. After the treatment Darin would walk to the car sick, not speaking a word. He just wanted to get home to his bedroom.

There was no cooking on the day of Darin's treatment because the smell of food made him even sicker. Darin knew that God was going to heal him.

In the beginning, he told his siblings, "No one is getting my bed, so don't get any ideas."

One morning during prayer God spoke to me, confirming He would heal my son. I rose from my knees, ran upstairs, and told Darin what God had spoken. In the midst of keeping up with his college aeronautical engineering classes and all the chemo treatments, Darin proposed to his sweetheart, Monica, on Valentines Day. They planned a wedding for November.

During this time, Barb and I were invited by a senior brother in the ministry to attend a two-month theological course in Coventry, England. We desired to go, but were hesitant to leave Darin. The course was being given one time during July and August.

Darin insistently encouraged us to go, saying, "I'm feeling much better and God will take care of me."

I will be strong and my heart will take courage.
(Psalm 27:14)

By June, Darin's eighth month of chemotherapy, he was handling the treatments without help from me, so Barb and I agreed to leave for the theological course. While studying in England, a teacher who taught the first session of the day made it known that, while in prayer that morning, God told him that He was going to heal a relative of someone studying in that class. In response, Barb and I raised our hands and the brother prayed for Darin and others.

We called home on Monday and Tuesday, but there was no answer. On Wednesday, I spoke with our daughter who told us Darin was in a lot of pain and his right arm was swollen.

On Thursday, I spoke with Darin who told us, "I have great news! The doctor said there's no more cancer in my body so he's taking me off Chemotherapy."

"Son, they can't do that," I replied and asked about the pain and the swelling in his arm.

Darin said, "It's only because a nurse administered something in my arm incorrectly."

I got the telephone number of the doctor, and after a lengthy discussion with him, was convinced God had miraculously healed our son. Not only was Darin free of cancer, he had also finished all his college courses. I knew once again God's hand was upon our family.

I am the Lord who heals you. (Exodus 15:26)

In mid-July, Darin graduated from St. Louis University. Barb and I were saddened that we were not there to congratulate our son for all his hard work during the most difficult time of his life. Darin's siblings and Barb's parents stood in for us at the ceremony.

Upon completing the theological course, we stayed in England to build a large wooden deck at the college. Barb helped me in the construction project for a couple of months and then returned to

St. Louis. I completed the project and returned home for Darin's wedding. On November 10, all who knew Darin and Monica celebrated with them at their wedding. It was a celebration of defeating the enemy and of God uniting two precious young people together in marriage.

After the wedding, I got back into the groove of traveling on the road every other week. In early December, it was my week to go to Florida. As I was driving through Georgia, praying and worshiping the Lord, I heard God say, "Give the business to your son." I heard it but didn't accept it as a word from the Lord. After a week of building new clients, I left Miami. Driving north on the way back home, I remembered a phone conversation earlier that week with Don Jr. He had said he wanted to be set free to build his own business. I kept thinking about that, hoping he wouldn't leave me.

About fifty miles north of Miami, I saw an automobile down in a gulley with a woman and a child standing next to it and a man on the highway, hitchhiking. I pulled over to see if I could help. I thought I could take him to the next exit to get help, so I opened the door and the man got in. I couldn't understand his Spanish and I smelled liquor on the man. The hitchhiker recognized a worship tape I was playing when he heard the name, "Jesus." I asked him where he needed to go, but sadly, I didn't understand him. I remembered the woman and the child back at the abandoned car, but couldn't find out who they were or what they needed.

Then I heard a little voice whisper, "Give him $25.00."

I said, "I'm not giving him any money, he'll just drink it up."

Driving more than a hundred miles north, the hitchhiker remained calm. I asked him several times where he needed to get out, but I couldn't understand him.

Each time I asked him, the same little voice said, "Give him $25.00."

Three times that happened and finally the hitchhiker motioned for me to stop and again the little voice said, "Give him $25.00."

Finally, I said, "Okay, but he's Your responsibility if he drinks it all up."

I gave him the $25.00. Thanking me, the man got out and I drove on. I never found out what happened to him or the woman and child. Back on the highway, I started praying for God to set the hitchhiker free from alcohol.

"Fear not, you worm Jacob, you men of Israel! I will help you," says the LORD. (Isaiah 41:14)

While driving, God spoke to me again and said, "Give the business to your son. If you believe I will take care of the hitchhiker, then believe I will also take care of your son."

I spoke to God saying, "Don Jr. doesn't know how to lead a business."

God said, "You didn't either when you first started."

I said, "He's too young!"

God said, "You were the same age when you started your barbershop."

Then I said, "But he has no money."

God said, "You didn't have any money either when you started."

Finally, I said, "But he has an attitude sometimes."

God said, "That's because he wants and needs more responsibility."

I returned home on Friday night and had no communication over the weekend with Don Jr. Normally, Monday morning we would meet for prayer at 7:00 a.m., but on this Monday morning, Don Jr. wasn't there. Then about 7:15 a.m., I heard the office door open. After about twenty minutes, it opened again, and I saw him leaving.

"Wait a minute son, I have a question for you. What do you want to do with your life?"

He looked at me and said, "I want to help you build this company."

"Okay, son, please sit down. I have something to tell you."

I told him of my argument with God and said, "Therefore, come January 1, you will be leading this business. There is only one stipulation to this important decision. This company will support your mom and me for the rest of our lives. In thirty days, I'll be out, and you'll be in."

We hugged each other and thanked each other for our working relationship. I retired from the company I loved so much on December 31, 1989. I continued to travel and build a new business but did not have the daily operating responsibilities of the company. I experienced several months of tranquility.

At midnight, in May of the following year, while Barb and I were sleeping, the phone rang. As I answered it, I heard sirens and saw flashing red lights in my mind from police cars and an ambulance.

Then a voice said, "Is this Mr. Kassebaum?"

"Yes, it is," I replied.

"You need to come to the hospital. Your son, Derrik, has been in a serious auto accident and he is just now being transported by ambulance."

On the way out the door, I explained what I knew to Barb and went to the hospital crying, praying, and trusting God. Barb arrived soon after. The doctor came out as she joined me in the emergency room lobby.

"It's possible we might need to remove his spleen," the surgeon explained.

I replied, "No, he came into this world complete, and when he leaves this world he'll leave complete. I'll not give permission."

We stayed the night and the next two days. Derrik was put in intensive care and after three days he was showing great progress.

Your enemies shall come out against you one way and flee before you seven ways. (Deut. 28:7)

My mind was occupied by thoughts of my son's recovery and my upcoming business travels. Barb and I agreed I needed to leave. Early the next week, I was on the east coast speaking with new clients. I called home frequently and each time received good news about Derrik. He spent two weeks in the hospital recuperating from the internal injuries. It wasn't long before he completely recovered.

Move to England

A year after Derrik's accident, Barb and I were asked to pray about coming to live in England to prepare young people to work among the poor in under-developed countries.

When I received this request from the senior brother in the ministry, I responded, "We don't need to pray about this. We know it's God's will for us and it's the desire of our heart. We will come."

"Great, we will prepare for your arrival," the brother responded.

By late spring, Barb and I prepared for our move to England. We had done some remodeling on our house and put it on the market for sale. Our vehicles were given into the business. And the church prayed and prophesied over us.

The day arrived for us to leave family and home. With six large suitcases to check at the airport and four to carry on the plane, the chaos began. Some of the suitcases exceeded weight limits, so we needed to transfer heavy items to the lighter bags. It was hot work.

With a nine-hour flight ahead of us and a screaming baby in the seat behind us, we began our travel with much frustration. Arriving in England, we rejoiced that the screaming had ended, but then discovered no one had been sent to pick us up at the airport. We had several hours to sit and relax, waiting for a ride. At last, a wonderful brother came to meet us and take us to the college.

At dinner that evening, we learned we were being asked to accept the position of administrators at the college. Seeking God's guidance on what to do, we found no peace in accepting this position. Then another opportunity came to us to administrate the ministry's yearly Bible week. We felt a need to accept this challenge to bless the brothers but felt rejected, homesick, and in need of God's direction. Back home, our house wouldn't sell. Without selling our house, we wouldn't be able to purchase a home or even a car in England.

After two and a half months in England, I had an appointment to meet with the senior brother. I was told we should return to the states because there was no longer a place for us in their ministry. As I left the office and got in the car with Barb, we both began laughing. We were going home.

Traveling three hours back to Keighley, I asked Barb, "What was the word that God gave you about coming to England?"

She said, "What word? I didn't receive a word. I thought you received God's word for us to be here."

I responded, "I didn't receive a word. I just wanted to come, and I thought it was God's will."

The next day our good friend, Don Silber, came to where we were staying. I asked him about what to do. Should we stay in England or should we go home?

He told us, "Don't go home unless you hear from God and don't stay here unless you hear from God. To hear God, you must be led by His Holy Spirit."

Carl and Barb Ropp, friends of ours, allowed us to use their home in Coventry while they were on vacation. It was a perfect place where we could be alone with God and pray. The first morning there, after a time of prayer and reading God's Word, we visited the city of Rugby. We spent the morning walking around and talking about what we saw God doing in our lives.

Leaving Rugby in the early afternoon, we returned to the house in Coventry. Barb began to prepare dinner and after reading the Word, I fell asleep on the couch. When I woke up four hours later, a word came to me: "Give careful thought to your ways." I thought, *Where is that in the Bible?* Opening up God's Word, I found it.

This is what the Lord Almighty says: "Give careful thought to your ways. You expected much, but see, it turned out to be little. What you brought home, I blew away. Why?" declares the Lord Almighty. "Because my house remains a ruin, while each of you is busy with his own house." (Haggai 1:7-9) NIV

I called Barb into the living room and said, "Listen to what I just received from the Lord."

I read the passage of scripture and said, "We've been here building our own ministry. I know if we return up north to Keithley and serve the brothers unquestionably, doing all they ask us to do, possibly in four or five years they will recognize our faithfulness to them and send us off to Africa to work as missionaries in an underdeveloped country."

Barb gave me a serious look and said, "Then who are we trying to please, the brothers or God?"

Immediately, I sought God's forgiveness and then we prayed for God's direction, promising Him, we would never make another major life decision without hearing from Him first.

On Sunday, we walked around the park for about two hours. It was just the medicine we needed. The weather was beautiful, and the presence of God was more so. Looking to the Lord and not to man was so refreshing to our souls. We were set free that Sunday morning from the religious activities we were normally involved in and excited we were going home. We came to England because of our own errors, made by our own decisions, and not by anyone else's. God was with us and we knew it. He would guide us if we seek Him first.

That afternoon we found flights back to the states at half the cost of our flights coming over. Leaving England, we were prepared with the proper weight of luggage. The flight was so peaceful. God was with us. When the plane set down on the runway in St. Louis, we knew we were home. Our family came to welcome us. What a homecoming it was. Our hearts were full of joy.

Opening the door of the house we knew so well, we were so grateful to God for His provision. It looked so beautiful to us. We were only gone for a few months, but we learned so much.

Our home had been on the market to sell for many months. The day after we returned we took it off. Within a week of being home, the same real estate company called to ask if they could list it again. They thought they had a buyer for it, but we told them no. We were tired of the frustration. The agent then asked if we would list it for just one day. We agreed and the home sold. Nearly nine months on the market and it wouldn't sell, yet, in one day, the house sold. I knew it was because we were once again in the will of God.

Guatemala

We continued to seek God's direction for our lives. We now had equity in our account and free time on our hands. God had put it on our hearts to study Spanish. So, I contacted the National School of Language in Antiqua, Guatemala. We inquired if we could start school at the beginning of January. We were accepted and, once again, it was time to travel through Mexico and on to Guatemala. We began preparing to move out of our house in Chesterfield, Missouri. We rented a doublewide storage building and began boxing our belongings.

On December 26, with help from friends and family, we moved out of our home. Everything was put in the rented storage building. It was just the two of us in that large, empty house. Coming in from outside, I couldn't find Barb.

I called out to her and heard a little muttering from the master bedroom. As I entered, I saw Barb sitting on the floor crying. She had all her little keepsakes on the floor around her. That's all she had left from all those years of serving the Lord with me. Everything else was packed away and put in storage. She no longer had a home for her family to visit. I just sat down on the floor with her and held her tight.

> *Everyone who has left houses or brothers or sisters or father or mother or children or fields for my sake will receive a hundred times as much and will inherit eternal life.* (Matthew 19:29) NIV

We had no idea that at this time a new ministry was being birthed. Many years later, we could look back and see how God had blessed us throughout the years and built a ministry that we could never have built on our own.

For our drive to Guatemala, we purchased a 1979 International Diesel Scout. Not much to look at, but it was strong and tough and had a lot of power. Mexican roads were rough with more potholes than pavement. Five to twenty miles per hour was as fast as we were able to travel in many areas. On December 27, we left our home in the states and headed south to Guatemala in our brown and white Scout.

We stayed in the same motel in Tampico as before and the next day we drove to Vera Cruz. It was New Year's Eve with beautiful weather and a night of celebration with Mexican music. The next day, we drove south and stayed for two nights in a beautiful motel in Catemaco, Mexico. On January 3, we arrived at the Guatemalan border at 8:00 a.m. By 9:30 a.m., we were totally cleared and approved to pass into Guatemala. It was a six-hour trip to the orphanage, "Casa Bernabe." We arrived there mid-afternoon and met with our church team from the United States.

That same day, I met with Quique Cazali, a young pastor raising up a new church in San Pedro Pinula, a village in the mountains around Jalapa, Guatemala. I had met Quique while serving in Casa Barnabe a few years earlier. Quique was preparing for the long six-hour bus ride to Pinula, where he lived. He was a man that would lay down his life for whoever needed help. He became a great friend to me.

I volunteered to drive Quique to his house in Pinula that night. The trip was a three-hour journey by car and my first experience of driving the highways of Guatemala at night. Four-wheel drive was needed for more than an hour on the last twelve miles before arriving in Pinula. When we arrived at Quique's home, we were introduced to his lovely wife, "Carolina." She was so beautiful and hospitable. Quique introduced us as his spiritual parents as well.

As many as are led by the Spirit of God, these are sons of God. (Romans 8:14)

I was asked to preach at Quique's church on Sunday morning but declined because of our schedule, but I promised to return on the next weekend. On Saturday morning, we left Quique and Carolina to return to Casa Bernabe. We stayed there two nights and worked with the team from our home church. On Monday morning, we drove to Antiqua to begin studying Spanish. One requirement of studying Spanish in Antiqua is to live in a house with a Spanish family. No English was allowed. We were assigned to live with a family in a truly Spanish setting and a friendship grew.

Years passed so quickly, they seemed like mere months as we learned about missionary life in underdeveloped nations. Each day brought new training that created new life. During the training, we discovered it wasn't easy to be away from our family. It was the biggest hurdle of all to climb.

We were always invited to stay as guests in the homes of the poor and needy. It was a real awakening as to what was the normal life in Guatemala. Gradually, we learned the eternal blessings of God in each situation.

Another day was about to dawn at the university of faith, hope, and love. God had His agenda for us at the borders and on the highways of Mexico, Guatemala, El Salvador, Honduras, and Nicaragua. Fortunately, we would meet God's servants and helpers along the way.

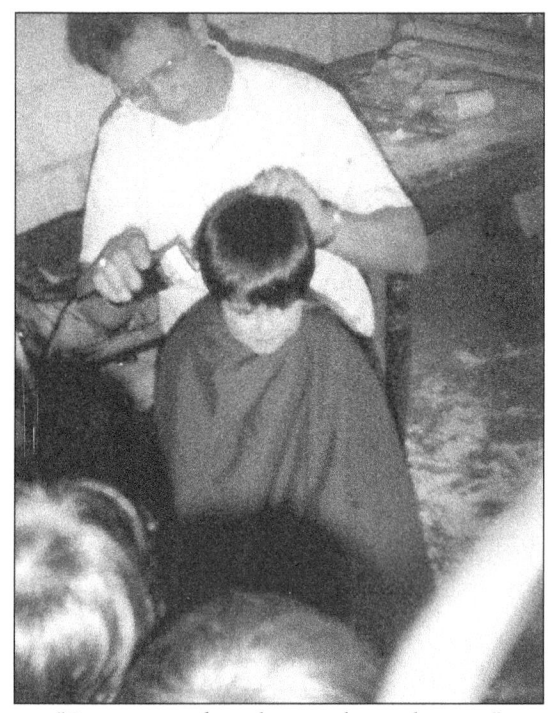

"Don cutting boys hair in the orphanage."

"Team members working on construction of orphanage."

Chapter 3

ANGELS FOLLOW US

Therefore I tell you, whatever you ask for in prayer, believe that you have received it, and it will be yours. (Mark 11:24) NIV

We were excited about studying Spanish. Arriving at the school, we met our personal tutors. We studied four hours a day but soon increased it to six. During break time, we enjoyed the bakery goods at Cinderella Pastries. After class, we would go to the park and try to use the Spanish we were learning with children, who were always trying to sell us something.. When I wouldn't buy anything, they began to call me, "El Cheapo." I thought, *Is that real Spanish?*

During class one Friday morning, I learned of a man who had just been put in jail. He was driving a bus near the site where someone was killed in an accident. He happened to be in the wrong place at the wrong time. When I heard about this, my tutor and I prayed for the man to be released from jail. We decided to go and visit him. Arriving at the jail, we discovered that the man had just been released. We rejoiced for what God had done for the bus driver.

Barb and I left school on a Friday for San Pedro Pinula, where I was to preach on Sunday. The next morning after breakfast we were told we were going to the church, to prepare for a service that night. Arriving, we saw a rough dirt floor and only one half of a roof covered with tin and no windows or doors. There was no electricity, no water, and of course, no bathroom.

I was asked to tape about thirty, six-foot long, two-strand electrical wires together. They gave me one small roll of black tape. I was supposed to tape all these pieces together to make one long wire. I gave a young boy some money to buy six more small rolls of black tape. An hour later the boy returned with only one roll. So, I started to join the many pieces of wire together with the tape I had. When I finished, I had made a 200-foot extension cord, yet never ran out of tape.

That evening all was ready for the service. The long extension cord was strung across the ground, up through a tree, across the road, and into an outlet on a building. It worked!

Prior to the service, it started raining. Looking outside, I saw the electric cord running in and out of puddles of water during a downpour of rain. Looking at the metal microphone, I thought, *Who's going home first tonight to be with the Lord.* I tapped on the microphone to see if I would be shocked. It looked to everyone else like I was testing it to see if it was working. All appeared to be working fine.

As I preached, an interpreter translated. She knew a little English and I knew a little Spanish. While I preached, she seemed to be doing pretty good. I thought, *Maybe she's preaching her own message.*

There was a man at the meeting that appeared intoxicated as he stood up and began talking very loudly. I didn't understand him and tried to get him to sit down, but he only got louder. Quique motioned to me that the man wanted to receive Jesus in his life. With that, the meeting ended, and many prayed for this man as he gave his life to Jesus. He was my first convert and I was grateful that God used me in that way. After two great days in Pinula, Barb and I needed to return to Antiqua.

Time to Return to the U.S.

Three months of Spanish classes passed quickly, and it was time to return home to the U.S.A. Leaving Antiqua early, we arrived at the northern Guatemala border. After turning in all our paperwork, the one arm gate lifted, and we left Guatemala. Arriving at the Mexican immigration office, we discovered Mexico had adopted a new immigration law. For a foreigner to drive a vehicle through Mexico, a U.S. auto insurance policy needed to be in the vehicle. With much persistence, I tried to get our Mexican paperwork legalized but failed.

Finally, I picked up all my papers and returned to the vehicle and told Barb, "They won't let us into Mexico. We need to return to Guatemala."

Returning to the Guatemala border, I talked the gatekeeper into raising the one-arm gate for us to pass through. I then went to the same office as before. Seeing my paperwork sitting on the corner of a clerk's desk, I picked it up and walked out of the office. No one said a word. Crossing the street, I got back into the Scout and drove off. Not knowing what to do, I just kept driving. At one point, I stopped to look at the map and saw another border town about three hours' drive through the mountains and decided to go there.

Coming around a sharp curve, I saw a large piece of lumber stretched across the mountain road. It had big nails sticking up through it. Stopping, a man with an ugly black hood covering his face came to the car window wanting money.

I said, "No understand."

The man said, "Money Señor."

When I opened my wallet, the man took all the money that was in it. The man motioned for other men at the barricade to pull it out of the way. We were then allowed to pass through. We never carried much money on our personal possessions; therefore, could not lose much.

The steps of a good man are ordered by the Lord.
(Psalm 37:23)

We followed the map and three hours later arrived at another border. Walking through the office area, I heard a buzzing about the new law in Mexico for U.S. travelers: "No U.S. auto insurance – No travel through Mexico." I drove the Scout directly in front of the exit gate that was lifted. I handed our passports and paperwork to an officer who began looking through them. Then another officer came, and it appeared that they were arguing whether we could pass or not.

The engine was running, and the doors were open. I gently took all the paperwork from the hand of the first officer and told Barb to quietly get back in the vehicle and not slam the door shut. When she was in, I slowly walked to the driver's door, got in the vehicle, put it in gear, released the brake, and proceeded to drive forward ever so slowly with my door slightly open. Watching through the rearview mirrors, I kept advancing forward. When they were completely out of sight, I closed my door and thanked God for helping us cross the border.

We drove for about thirty minutes into Tapachula, Mexico. There we found an attorney's office to seek advice about driving back to the U.S. through Mexico. The attorney was out to lunch but was expected to return soon. We had all our paperwork ready when we entered his office. We were told we needed someone in the states to fax down our U.S. auto insurance policy. There was an office supply store next to his office where we spoke to a young girl about our predicament. She was very kind and said we could use her telephone and fax machine to receive our U.S. Auto Insurance Policy. Being late in the day her store was closing, but she assured us she would be in by eight in the morning. So, we acquired a hotel room for the night and after dinner, rested.

In the morning we were at the office supply store early, waiting for the young girl to return to receive our paperwork. When she arrived, she gave us the auto insurance policy and offered to guide us through the city of Tapachula to the office of immigration. We were praying all the way, asking the Lord to help us pass through. Arriving there she waved goodbye. She was a gift from God.

Do not forget to entertain strangers, for by so doing some people have entertained angels without knowing it. (Hebrews 13:2 NIV)

An officer looked through our paperwork and said, "Yes, it all seems in order."

He stamped it, we paid our fee of $15.00 and were on our way through Mexico. We began singing and praising God with all our hearts.

During our time in Guatemala, many highways in southern Mexico were resurfaced. The drive was beautiful, and by 5:00 p.m. we stopped at a hotel for the night. Early the next morning, we were back on the same rough roads we knew from before. As in the past, five miles an hour in some areas was the limit because of potholes. When we arrived at the U.S. border, there was no problem crossing. Driving on U.S. highways again was such a blessing.

Arriving back in St. Louis with no home to return to, we looked for a place to live. A real estate agent we knew began showing us different homes to rent or purchase. The first home we saw that day we liked very much. By the end of the day, we made an offer on it. It was the same amount our previous home sold for. The seller accepted our offer and we had ourselves another house.

After moving into our new home, I began raising money for our upcoming travels by building decks and painting houses. I enjoyed working with my hands, so this turned out to be a blessing to me.

Nicaragua

After many months of raising money for our mission work, Geoff, a friend of mine, asked me if I would be available to drive a Scout to an orphanage in Nicaragua. Excitement began to rise in my heart to do this. Barb reminded me of my promise to God, to seek Him before making any major decision. We began to pray about this challenge.

We left our home for a while to be alone with God. We drove out West towards Wyoming while praying about the trip to Nicaragua. One evening on an elevator at a hotel in Wyoming, God spoke to me about driving Geoff's vehicle south. When I told Barb, she began to cry. She just needed to know God was with us. The Holy Spirit then smothered us with His love and peace. By the end of July, we had left our home in Wildwood to drive Geoff's Scout to Nicaragua.

Arriving at the U.S./Mexican border, we learned we had a three-day waiting period to cross into Mexico because the vehicle was going only one-way. On the fourth day, we were released to leave the border and join a convoy. I couldn't believe I needed to follow this convoy all the way to Guatemala. So, I passed all the vehicles and we were on our way again.

As we arrived in Tampico around 2:30 p.m., we searched for an elder from a church we had been told to visit if ever there. After finding Elder Juan Manual, we were invited to stay in his home and dine with them that evening. Four other elders joined us and began to ask me many questions about my beliefs. I enjoyed the discussion. As the evening enshrouded us on that Saturday night, I was invited to preach in the first meeting in the morning. In that service, all five elders were there to listen. They were all standing along the walls in the outer aisles. They were true pastors, protecting their sheep. I was then asked to take the second meeting. I loved it. The day was full of good time and laughter.

On Monday morning, we were up by 5:00 a.m., as usual, to leave for Southern Mexico. Just prior to leaving Juan Manual's home, his wife, Anjelica, gave Barb a gift. It was a pair of shoes purchased the day before for Anjelica. Barb, thinking they were a family of meager income, told them she could not accept such an important gift. They pleaded for her to take it. I also urged Barb to take the gift, and she did with tears in her eyes. As we were leaving Tampico, we were both crying because of the love shown to us by the people of the church.

It was a long day of driving south. We stayed in a hotel in Catemaco, south of Vera Cruz, for two nights. We left the hotel on Wednesday morning to travel to Tecum Uman, where we arrived the next day. There was much bureaucracy at the border, and we needed to pass through thirteen offices for different paperwork. Each office required a payment of money. I hired a ten-year-old boy, Benny, to help us through each office.

Before leaving home, I hid a sewing machine in the back of the Scout. I was also carrying many schoolbooks. At the border, I was required to unload everything from the vehicle, even in the rain. For some reason, the sewing machine had disappeared. I didn't understand it and was also concerned for the books. After the inspection, officials told me to put everything back. Later that night when I was unloading the vehicle, the sewing machine was right in the same place I had put it back home. I know it was an angel of the Lord that hid it.

No weapon formed against you shall prosper; And every tongue that rises against you. . .you shall condemn. (Isaiah 54:17)

It was dark by the time we left the border. Benny got in the car to guide us to a hotel, "The Virginian," about one hour away. Arriving there, I went in to acquire a room, while Barb and Benny kept talking together. He told Barb his parents were killed one year ago in an auto accident. He lived with his sister and tried to earn money each day at the border to support the two of them. He saw a Bible on the dashboard of the car and asked if he could have it.

"Yes, of course," Barb said.

She also gave him a nice tip for helping them during the day.

Inspecting the hotel room, I found it to be a clean, basic room. Then in the hotel restaurant, we listened to a group traveling to the Capitol City. I asked them if I could join their convoy. They agreed if we could be ready by 4:00 a.m.

Early the next morning, we were ready. After driving for about an hour, there was a police roadblock. Five of the six cars in the convoy was pulled over for inspection of passports, license, and vehicle paperwork. Our car and the one in front of us passed through. A few blocks away, we stopped and waited for the other five cars to be released. It wasn't long before we were all on the road again.

A week passed as we tried to get someone to travel with us to Nicaragua, but I failed. So, on Friday, we drove to San Pedro Pinula to visit with Quique and Carolina. In Pinula, I enjoyed fellowship with some brothers at a leadership breakfast. After giving a short report of our travels and preaching on Sunday, we left early Monday morning for El Salvador.

We arrived at the El Salvador border and began the process of passing through many offices to leave Guatemala. There was a cost from each office to get border-crossing approval. Finishing this process, I walked a long distance to the El Salvador border. Arriving at the immigration office, I was told we needed visas to enter El Salvador. This meant we needed to return to Guatemala to acquire our visas and would lose the money we paid earlier to leave Guatemala. For the five-hour drive back to Guatemala, I would need to drive at night, which was very dangerous for a foreigner. I pleaded with the officials but with no success.

After retrieving all of our paperwork, I walked the long distance back to our vehicle where Barb was waiting. I told Barb what had happened. Not knowing what to do, we prayed asking for God's help and wisdom.

The effective, fervent prayer of a righteous man avails much. (James 5:16)

When we finished praying, I looked up at the El Salvador border, about two blocks away, and saw a man waving at someone down at the Guatemala border. I looked at the hundreds of people around there but saw no one waving back. Two more times I saw the man waving, so I waved back and the man kept waving. I then walked up the hill to the El Salvador border and recognized the brother from the preceding weekend at the Saturday morning leadership breakfast in San Pedro Pinula.

Filled with joy to see Roberto, I called him an Angel of the Lord. When I explained all that had happened, Roberto took all our paperwork and returned to the same office and spoke to the same people I had spoken to before. Within fifteen minutes and paying $35.00 for each visa, we had all the paperwork and visas we needed. We followed Roberto and were on our way to San Salvador to meet with other brothers from one of the Verbo churches we had a relationship with.

When I attended the church council meeting there, it was decided Roberto would go with us to help drive and navigate our way to Nicaragua. On August 18, our thirtieth wedding anniversary, the three of us left San Salvador and headed to Honduras and then to Nicaragua.

God blessed our Honduras border crossing. With time running short to arrive at the Nicaragua border before it closed for the day, Roberto told me to drive quickly through an upcoming intersection that had a stop sign. Immediately, a policeman waved his hands for me to stop and asked me for my license. When I gave it to him, the officer in his small hut, threw it in his desk drawer and told us we would need to return to the border to regain it. Roberto pleaded for the license to be returned. The officer appeared to be getting angry. He finally opened his desk drawer and took the license out and threw it at me. I handed the ticket back to the policeman and walked out the door. We began racing to the Nicaragua border which was to close at 4:00 p.m.

Arriving at 4:05 p.m., God's favor was with us once again. Roberto handled all the paperwork while I went out to the car to wait with Barb.

I put my head in the window and said, "Well, once again, a little bit of bad news."

"What now?" Barb asked.

"We need to return to El Salvador because some papers were filled out improperly," My shoulders were slumped and I looked down.

"Oh, no, I can't believe it. I'm tired of all this hassle," Barb replied angrily. "I just want a shower and a bed to sleep in."

Realizing she was not at all happy about what I said, I told her the truth, "I'm sorry, there's no problem. The paperwork is almost completed and we'll be on our way in a few minutes."

Barb was in no mood for my attempted humor.

We soon arrived in Managua, met the brothers, and then went to the orphanage. Since there was no hot water there for a shower, we decided to get a hotel for the night. Upon arriving at 8:30 p.m., there was a welcoming party awaiting us. They were so kind and friendly.

I asked, "Is there hot water for a shower?"

They replied, "Natural."

Oh boy, what am I going to tell Barb? I thought.

The people were too nice to just leave so we took our showers in water, "Natural," which meant, not cold, not hot.

On Thursday, August 20, Barb flew home for her parent's fiftieth wedding anniversary. I gave the Scout to the orphanage and on Friday a church team from the U.S. arrived to finish the construction of a small warehouse building, and to wash all the children's hair with a shampoo for head lice.

One day while eating some watermelon across the table from a girl, we suddenly saw a black seed apparently stand up and walk across her piece of watermelon. We looked at each other and started laughing and then got up and threw our plates of watermelon into the trash can. She went back and got another piece, but I never ate another piece of watermelon while in Nicaragua. The church team completed their ten days of service and we all returned to the states.

Hurricane Andrew

A few days after arriving home, hurricane Andrew struck Miami, Florida, bringing much devastation. Hundreds of mobile homes were blown away, many homes were destroyed, and thousands of roofs demolished. Victims were without food, clothing, and personal belongings. Sixty-five deaths were reported, and hundreds of injured people were hospitalized. Thousands of lives were shattered. As we watched the news, our hearts were torn.

I know that the Lord will maintain the cause of the afflicted. (Psalm 140:12)

We talked with Pastor Geoff as to the possibility of moving to Florida to help alleviate the trauma the hurricane had caused. Geoff was thrilled to hear we wanted to go and spoke with a pastor in Miami about sending us there to lead a work team in helping the victims of the hurricane.

We were soon on our way to Miami. Upon arriving, we met Tono, the pastor of a Verbo church already serving the victims. Land was loaned to them and donations were flowing in. Nineteen young Guatemalan adults traveled through Mexico to help serve, plus five North Americans joined us. The U.S. Army donated eight, fifteen-man tents that were set up for all who came to serve.

As soon as the Guatemalans and North Americans arrived the work began. Each day started with one hour of corporate prayer, worship, and the word at 6:00 a.m. Donations came from the U.S. Army, the United Way, the Salvation Army, and private donors. I met with a Colonel from the U.S. Army nearly every other day to review the many needs that were before us. A large vacant building was donated to be used as a warehouse and distribution center. Some of the young Guatemalans were used as translators for government projects. Teams were set up for kitchen staff, construction work, office details, and evangelistic outreaches. Hot showers were acquired by running water through 250 feet of one-inch black tubing, laying on hot sand in the hot sun. Barb and I coordinated the work.

One day my friend, Carlos and I went to receive thirty mattresses from a donor. They were all loaded on an open truck and secured with rope. It started raining halfway back to the mission center and the rope broke holding the mattresses, as we were driving across a large river bridge. Mattresses began flying off the truck all over the interstate. Carlos stopped and we began chasing mattresses in the middle of rain and traffic. By God's grace, there were no accidents and all the mattresses were retrieved.

Working with the young adults, I learned the value of prayer before the meetings began and also when decisions needed to be made to avoid arguments.

At the end of the six-month Miami mission project, the distribution center was still full of building materials, tools, medical supplies, furniture, clothing, and canned food. We contacted churches and organizations throughout the U.S. looking for interest in covering shipping charges to send a forty-foot container of aid to needy nations. Our staff would load it with aid. In the end, the mission sent out twenty-two 40-foot containers of aid around the world. We also had three trucks that were to be given to other charitable works in South Dade, Florida. The money that was left in the Hurricane Andrew bank account was sent to charitable organizations in various South American countries.

When it was time to return home, the Guatemalans were heading to California to work with another ministry. They asked us to accompany them, but that wasn't possible at that time. We followed them as far as Dallas, helping them when their bus broke down in Oklahoma.

After three weeks of rest and seeking to hear from God, I had a vision while driving through Utah, singing and praying. I saw a picture hanging on a wall filled with items of furniture, food, money, vehicles, medical supplies, and physical aid for the needy.

God said, "This is what you will do with your life. You will gather in what I give you and send it out to those in need."

Whoever is kind to the needy honors God.
(Proverbs 14:31 NIV)

We traveled back home excited about what God had in store for us. I began building decks and painting houses to support our upcoming travel needs. I was seeking the Lord to return to San Pedro Pinula, but Barb didn't agree that the time was right.

One morning in the shower, praying for direction, God spoke, "Not Now!"

Without knowing it, the church in Pinula was almost completely dissolved because of a cult putting lies into church members minds, but God's plan was unfolding. Several months later, God put it on our hearts to study more Spanish. We recognized how bad our Spanish was while working with the Guatemalans in Miami. So, we made plans to return for more study. When our church heard we were leaving to study more Spanish, they gave us an offering for our travel.

A few miles away from home as we began our trip to Guatemala, we heard a noise coming from the engine. Though I was concerned, I was determined to continue. The noise continued all the way to the Mexican border at Brownsville, Texas. We spent the night in Brownsville and crossed the border in the morning in route to Tampico. Shortly before arriving at Tampico, the generator failed. We continued to pray as I looked for a generator. I did not find one but did find a mechanic who improvised using a different model generator and it worked. God was with us.

As we left the hotel the next morning at 5:00 a.m., we encountered torrential rain and an increase in troublesome engine noise. After about two hours, we stopped and prayed.

Barb said, "Maybe there's a problem ahead we don't know about. Maybe God is warning us not to go on."

I agreed and headed back to the border. We prayed while driving for five hours towards the border. God moved.

Have no fear of sudden disaster or of the ruin that overtakes the wicked, for the Lord will be your confidence and will keep your foot from being snared. (Proverbs 3:25 NIV)

I told Barb I couldn't remember ever reading in the Bible where God told His people to turn back and not go forward. Just then I swerved to the left to avoid a huge chug hole. With that, the noise got very loud. When I did it again the same loud noise occurred, so I pulled onto the wide shoulder of the road and found a belt that was loose. It was difficult to see and worse to work on. I had to climb under the vehicle to tighten it. When the job was complete, there was no noise. We both praised the Lord for His watchful hand over our lives and headed back to Tampico for the night.

The next day we traveled south spending two nights and a day resting in Catemaco. As we continued south, the oil pressure gauge began to drop, and the lights went dim. There was no turning back to the U.S. border for Guatemala was much closer. We began praying for victory and God was again with us. As we prayed, the oil gauge went up and the lights got bright. When we stopped praying, the oil pressure dropped, and the lights grew dim. Once it was daylight, I was able to turn the lights and any electrical functions off. We kept praying and the vehicle kept moving. That night we stayed in a hotel in Tuxtla Gutiérrez.

We left the hotel at 4:00 a.m. and saw the appearance of a fire a long distance ahead of us. As we drove closer, we saw the fire was in a fifty-gallon drum and there were soldiers keeping warm around it. It was dark when the soldiers stopped us to search our vehicle. Finding no weapons, they let us pass. We arrived at the Guatemala border at 9:00 a.m. and within a short time were allowed to leave. We drove two full days praying the vehicle would not fail and it kept running.

Leaving the border, we drove toward Casa Bernabe Orphanage and stayed there for several nights until it was time to travel to Antiqua for three more months of studying Spanish. On weekends we drove to the church in San Pedro Pinula to preach and spend time with Quique and Carolina.

On our first weekend back in Pinula, the church had an anniversary dinner on Saturday night. As the ladies prepared the food, the men were setting up the building with tables and chairs. I saw a well-dressed man sitting over on the side by himself. I introduced myself and asked the man if he had been coming to the church for a long time.

The gentleman answered, "No, just for a few months."

I asked, "Have you been a Christian for a long time?"

The young man said, "No, just a few months."

Suddenly, I recognized the man. His name was Chepi. He was the drunk who received Jesus into his life during the first meeting I ever preached there. I was so thrilled to know that Chepi was a Christian. Nothing on earth was worth more than that experience.

At 4:00 a.m. Monday morning, we were back on the roads, headed for Antiqua. Traveling through Guatemala in a vehicle with U.S. license plates is like asking to be pulled over by the police. Once when we were stopped, the police concluded the car was not mine because it had a white roof. The title stated that it was a brown International Scout. They said they were going to confiscate the car. I prayed as I sat behind the steering wheel giving the car to God to do with as He pleased. A miracle happened: the police suddenly decided to let us go.

Miracles seemed to follow us as we lived life totally desiring to be in God's Will. To us, miracles are the normal way God lives in His people. We knew our task was only to believe.

This is the work of God, that you believe in Him whom He sent. (John 6:29)

Chapter 4

PERILOUS ENCOUNTERS!

The LORD will cause your enemies who rise against you to be defeated before your face; they shall come out against you one way and flee before you seven ways. (Deuteronomy 28:7)

We were in our second three-months of studying Spanish in Antiqua. We were enjoying life, being responsible only to ourselves. After breakfast each morning, we would walk to the school for Spanish classes. We each had our own tutor. A year and a half earlier, we had been told by the owner of the school that it would be very difficult for people over thirty-five to learn a new language unless they were already fluent in a second language. The reason was by the age of thirty-five, the mind is set only on one language and difficult to change the thinking process. We were older than forty-five, but I was determined to prove this theory wrong.

We continued our studies during the week and when we were not in San Pedro Pinula preaching on weekends, we visited other areas of interest. The scout was in need of much repair but was our only means of transportation. After three years of driving rough highways, it was ready for the salvage yard or a complete overhaul. We decided to rebuild the engine, replace the suspension, the body, and even the interior. It took about two months for the project to be completed. In the end, it looked and ran like a new vehicle. Rebuilding the Scout curtailed our travel to Pinula for many weeks so we were excited when we were able to get it back.

The time passed quickly and once again, we prepared for our return to the States. Our Spanish had greatly improved, but we still weren't fluent.

During our first visit to Guatemala, God spoke to us saying we would "go and come, go and come." We didn't understand exactly what that meant, but we held on to His Word.

Before leaving Guatemala, we met with the Director of the "Verbo Churches," Francisco Bianci, to seek counsel on how to serve the needy in Guatemala. He advised us to contact Mike Kadera, a U.S. missionary, who had served the poor in Guatemala for more than twenty years.

Your word is a lamp to my feet and a light to my path. (Psalm 119:105)

After leaving Francisco's office, we immediately contacted Mike. We knew the possibility of meeting with him was slim because we were leaving for the U.S. in the morning. However, when we spoke with him, we found him to be a very gracious man. He agreed to meet with us that evening.

Mike arrived at the home where we were staying and we shared our story with him. We told Mike the word God had given us during our first journey to Guatemala and asked him how we could serve the poor in this country. Mike gave us the simplest answer of all, and we knew it was straight from God. It brought excitement and joy to our hearts and would guide us throughout the rest of our lives.

It filled us with delight when he said, "Build on the word God already gave you. If you do, you will have success."

David behaved wisely in all his ways, and the LORD was with him. (1 Samuel 18:14)

The next morning, we found ourselves in extraordinary heavy traffic. It took two hours to get out of the city. Finally, we were on the highway leading northwest to the Mexican and Guatemalan border town of La Mesilla. We arrived there at midday and began the process of leaving Guatemala. We were released within an hour and arrived at the Mexican immigration and customs office shortly thereafter. It took only thirty minutes to be back on the road leading to the U.S. border, which was a four-day journey.

We stayed the night at a hotel in Tuxtla Gutiérrez, a town in southern Mexico. Early the next morning, we left the hotel at 4:00 a.m. to cross a mountain pass before the big trucks and buses began moving. Around 5:15 a.m., high on a mountain road, the accelerator pedal went to the floorboard and quit functioning. The motor would only idle. Using my flashlight, I started searching for the problem. Under the hood, I found that the accelerator cable had broken from the accelerator pedal. Barb took a flashlight and walked up the mountain road, around a hairpin curve, and out of sight in the darkness of the night to wave down trucks or buses that could be coming around that mountain curve. I used a pair of vice-grips and clamped the cable to the accelerator pedal which fixed the problem.

Once again we were on our way singing and praising God for all He had done for us. We stayed overnight in the same hotels we had used in the past. After four days of driving on Mexican highways, we arrived at the U.S./Mexico border. Crossing into the U.S. was quite easy and twenty-four hours later, we were home again.

During the next five months, we spent most of our time building decks and painting houses. When we needed more work, we would walk through the subdivision where we lived and put flyers on doorknobs, advertising for deck construction or painting jobs. Doing this brought us sufficient work.

Guatemalan Church Building Project

Shortly after Thanksgiving, our church had a team of twelve people going on a ten-day trip to Guatemala. They were to serve a church in Chimaltenango, a heavily populated town, at the base of several mountains. Their project was to construct a building that would house six classrooms for children's Sunday school. We knew God was calling us to return to Guatemala and begin building new relationships with pastors and their wives throughout many mountainous regions of the interior parts of Guatemala. As a result of our previous travels, we were better prepared for the unexpected.

We drove south to Laredo, Texas and then on to Monterrey, Mexico, meeting up with brothers of the Verbo church we had not met before. I shared God's Word with the church in Monterrey that evening and then we traveled north to Reynosa the next morning to share God's Word in another church later in the day. There were new converts and God healed, delivered, and restored new life to many.

Then we began our four-day journey south to Guatemala. One of those four days would be a day of rest. Our scout was running great and our travel through Mexico was going well until I went through a red light in Vera Cruz.

Let us come boldly to the throne of grace, that we may obtain mercy and find grace to help in time of need. (Hebrews 4:16)

The policeman at the corner of the intersection stopped me and asked for my license, passport, and the vehicle registration papers.

As I was putting it all together I heard the Holy Spirit say, "Ask what the cost of your error will be?"

I asked, "What is the cost of my error?"

The policeman told me the amount and I realized the same ticket in the U.S. would have cost much more. I asked if I could pay for the error at that time. The policeman agreed and we were on our way again.

Two days later, we arrived at the Guatemalan border. They went through all our paperwork and then we were free to enter

Guatemala by midday. It was a four-hour drive to Chimaltenango where we met up with the team from our church in the States. The building was well on its way to being completed. We joined the team led by our pastor, Geoff, and began helping with the project.

A month prior to our trip to Guatemala, a prophet came and spoke at our church on a Sunday morning. From the platform, he called Barb forward and proclaimed healing to her back, which brought instant healing. He then asked me to stand and he prophesied over me, saying God would speak through me before men in high positions. I never expected such an incredible word of opportunity. Yet, on that Friday afternoon in Guatemala, as the team was putting the finishing touches on their project, I was asked to come to "La Oficina del Alcalde," a government building in Chimaltenango.

About 3:00 p.m. I went with Geoff and two other brothers from the team to this huge government building. None of us knew where we were going because we did not understand the Spanish word, "Alcalde." Then I saw a plaque with that inscription on a beautiful desk. We discovered that the office we were in was the Mayor's office. Then I remembered the word the prophet spoke at our church in the States. It turned out I had the privilege of leading this man to the Lord. In his office, the Mayor wept, believing Jesus Christ died for his sins. This was another handwork of God using me for His purpose.

> *Therefore whoever confesses Me before men, him I will also confess before My Father who is in heaven.* (Matthew 10:32)

The team completed their project with excellence. The pastor and the team celebrated God's goodness on their last night in Guatemala. The next morning, the North Americans left for their homes in the States. Barb and I continued visiting churches in the interior, mountainous regions of Guatemala until the day came for us to return home to celebrate Christmas with our family. We put the scout in the long-term parking lot at the Guatemalan airport and flew home. Having a large family, we have always enjoyed coming together during the holidays. The time passed quickly and we returned to Guatemala in early January.

A few days after we arrived in Guatemala, I committed to being part of a medical team hiking through the mountains to villages where very few missionaries have ever gone. On this medical team, there were two doctors, three nurses, Tito, the team leader, and me.

The team left early on Friday from the Capitol City. We traveled in two cars for four hours to Coban, a beautiful city amid a scenic view of mountain ranges. Before boarding a small plane, each person needed to be weighed with our belongings. I weighed too much, so I needed to wait for the plane to return from transporting the first group of team members to the village of La Perla. While waiting, Tito and I went into town to purchase gas for the airplane. When we returned to the airport, the plane had arrived and the mechanic on sight siphoned the gas from the five-gallon cans into the gas tanks located in the wings of the small plane. I watched the whole ordeal. I thought, "Is this really the way they prepare a small plane for flight?"

After watching the plane being fueled, I walked around to the front and saw oil dripping from the engine onto the front tire.

I told the mechanic who responded, "Yeah, that's alright, we'll just put more oil in it."

I prayed, "Oh Lord, keep us safe in this time of need."

He is my refuge and my fortress; My God, in Him I will trust. (Psalm 91:2)

There was only one seat in the airplane, and it was for the pilot. Tito sat on the floor in the rear, facing the back of the plane. I sat on the floor facing the front of the plane with our backs leaned up against each other. My door was held shut by a piece of wire. When the pilot revved up the engine, I thought, *Every piece of metal on this plane might begin falling off. I hope the duct tape will hold.*

I was taking video and still photos of the beautiful picturesque view when fifteen minutes into the flight, I noticed the plane started to bank left heading back from where we came. The noise from the rattling of the plane metal was so loud, I could hardly hear what the pilot was saying.

I yelled, "What are you doing?"

The pilot said, "Going back to the airfield."

I asked, "Why?"

The pilot answered, "Because we can't make it over the mountain."

I began putting my cameras away and praying. When the plane landed, we unloaded everything and began looking for another plane. I suggested we pray. Shortly after praying, a beautiful, small plane landed.

Tito went out to the end of the runway to ask the pilot to take us and our supplies to La Perla. I saw the pilot shaking his head, "No." So I began praying for God's favor with this pilot. Within a few minutes, Tito came running back giving me the good news. We hurried back into the city to purchase more gas. After refueling the plane, loading the supplies, and climbing aboard, we were off again. In this plane, there were seats for everyone.

Landing on a mountaintop in La Perla, we met up with the rest of the team plus more than thirty locals from the village. We unloaded the supplies and began preparing to trek over the mountain ridge to Elim, the mountain village where the medical team would serve the natives. The locals carried all the supplies on their backs held on by a leather strap wrapped around their heads. Everyone carried something. I carried my camera case, a sleeping bag, and a backpack with personal items.

Upon leaving the mountaintop, I was the third person from the front of the line. Within about forty minutes, I was the tenth person from the front. One of the locals came and took my sleeping bag. After about another thirty minutes, someone else came and took my backpack. Those short, little guys were all passing me. After another fifteen minutes, a good Samaritan came and took my camera bag as many more passed me. Finally, another kind brother in the Lord came and gave me a towel soaked in cool water to hold over my head.

The team of nearly forty men climbed steep mountainsides and descended others. Whether ascending or descending it was all difficult for me. At one point, we needed to cross over a deep ravine walking on a round log used as a bridge from one side to the other.

Everyone made it and after a five-and-a-half-hour trek, we arrived safely in Elim. It was an extremely poor village with sewage running down the pathways in between the many metal huts. The women were afraid of me. I was told there had only been one other white man who ever came to their village. The team of seven began preparing for the medical clinic the next day.

Whatever you do, do it heartily, as to the Lord and not to men.
(Colossians 3:23)

After all, preparations were made, each one sprayed their sleeping bag with insect repellant and slept on a bench that night. When morning came, the doctors and nurses began their work. I was the pharmacist. Everyone received some type of pill or liquid medicine, even if it was only a sugar pill. By that evening, the women were beginning to trust me and even permitted photos. In the clinic, I witnessed the removal of a roach embedded in the ear of one of the patients. More than a 150 patients received medical help that day. The next morning, a service was held in their church building before the team began their long trek back to La Perla.

The return trek was even more difficult for me than the trek going into Elim two days prior. I began to get tired and wore out much faster. By the time we arrived in La Perla, I would count one hundred steps and then sit down to rest for a couple of minutes. When I arrived at the finish line, I was thrilled that all of us were safe and had accomplished our mission. It took two trips by the small plane to get everyone back to Coban and then on to Guatemala City. Everyone was pleased with what had been accomplished in the village of Elim over the past weekend.

I rested throughout the following week. Friday, I shared God's Word in a church in Jutiapa, located in the southern part of Guatemala. I was to speak in meetings for the next three evenings. Many responded to God's Word in each meeting creating a pathway for the movement of the Holy Spirit. Many came forward for healing and God responded to their hearts of sincerity. It was late when we returned to the pastor's house to rest for the night.

On Monday morning as we were preparing to return to the Capitol, news on the TV spoke about hurricane Mitch slamming the southern part of Guatemala. They were warning people not to drive on the highways unless it was absolutely necessary. I felt it was imperative we leave immediately.

Pablo, my translator, and Janet, a missionary from the U.S., joined Barb and me in the scout as we began our travel back to the Capitol City. Driving around hairpin curves on a mountainous highway in torrential rain was very dangerous. Coming around one of the sharp curves, I saw many people standing outside in the torrential rain. As I approached the curve, big rocks and clumps of mud began falling off the mountainside onto the scout.

Barb screamed, "Go, Go, Go."

With that incentive, I pushed the accelerator pedal down to go as fast as I could. We made it through the curve. As I looked back in my rearview mirror, I saw the highway giving way and most of it fell down the mountainside.

A month later, we were traveling along that same highway and saw the place where the highway had fallen away. There was a temporary bridge built in that same location. I could see how gracious our Heavenly Father had been that day of the storm. He has continuously protected us from the perils of the enemy.

We arrived in the Capitol City remembering God's promise to always go with us, never leaving nor forsaking us. The travel that should have taken two hours took more than five, thus, we were tired and needed to be with our family. We ventured out on these journeys because we knew God had a call on our lives. We also knew the importance of returning to our family from time to time. We knew it was time for us to head home.

Before leaving Guatemala, we stopped in San Juan Ostuncalco for the night. We stayed with Mario and Angelica Garcia, the pastors of the Verbo church. Mario asked me to go up into the mountains with him to pray for a leader of the church who was sick. I agreed, so the two of us walked for a long time and came to a small, concrete blockhouse that had one small living room with no furniture. It had two small bedrooms with only mattresses on the floor. The kitchen had a homemade concrete block wood stove, with a big piece of metal on the top where the cooking was done. The kitchen also had two box crates for chairs and some concrete blocks holding up a small piece of warped plywood for a table.

The only family member present was the wife of the church leader. She wore a beautiful smile and made us feel welcome with her coffee. I was crying on the inside asking God, *How can I help these poor people, Lord?*

After a short while, we knew it was time to leave. Before leaving, we prayed for the father and all his family.

As Mario and I walked back, I asked God again, *How can I help these poor people here, Lord?*

God said, "Go home and get a convoy of trucks filled with aid to help the poor in Guatemala."

I told Mario the word I just received.

Mario replied, "Wonderful!"

I felt a new, adventurous ministry was about to unfold. All this began because we stopped at the pastor's house for a night of rest before traveling onward in the morning.

> *"My word that goes out from my mouth: It will not return to me empty, but will accomplish what I desire and achieve the purpose for which I sent it."* (Isaiah 55:11 NIV)

The next day we left early, traveling south to Malacatán, crossing the border without problems.

While traveling that day, Barb said, "Don, wouldn't it be great to bring a group of trucks with aid to help the poor in Guatemala?"

Up to that moment, I had not spoken to her about the word I received in Ostuncalco. Now God was confirming His new ministry to us.

We spent the night in Catemaco, Mexico, with two or three more days of travel to reach the U.S. border. This gave us time to talk about the new adventure God was moving us into. By the time we finished our travel through Mexico and returned home in the U.S., our excitement had grown to new levels.

After being home for a few weeks, I began writing letters to many churches asking them to be part of a convoy of trucks taking aid to the poor in Guatemala. I sent out more than fifty letters and received only five responses. Of the five responses, there was one church in support of the project. It was the Abundant Life Church in Union, Mo. This was our home church. I called another friend who was pastoring a church in Florida. My friend had many good reasons why they couldn't be a part of this project and then gave me some great advice.

He said, "Why don't you consider filling a container full of aid and sending it to Guatemala?"

I thanked him for his advice and tried to forget it. I was discouraged and felt beat up inside after several days of calling pastors, and not receiving any positive commitments. The thought of using containers wasn't in my plan. The more I thought about it, the more irritated I was until one day I put my head in my hands, wept, and handed it all over to God.

"Using containers is Your idea God, not mine. If it fails, it's Your fault. It's all Yours, God. I will serve You in it anyway You direct me to serve. I give it all to You."

When I sat up, the pressure was gone and I felt free again. A new ministry had just been launched.

Perilous Encounters!

"Fueling Don's plane for medical mission team."

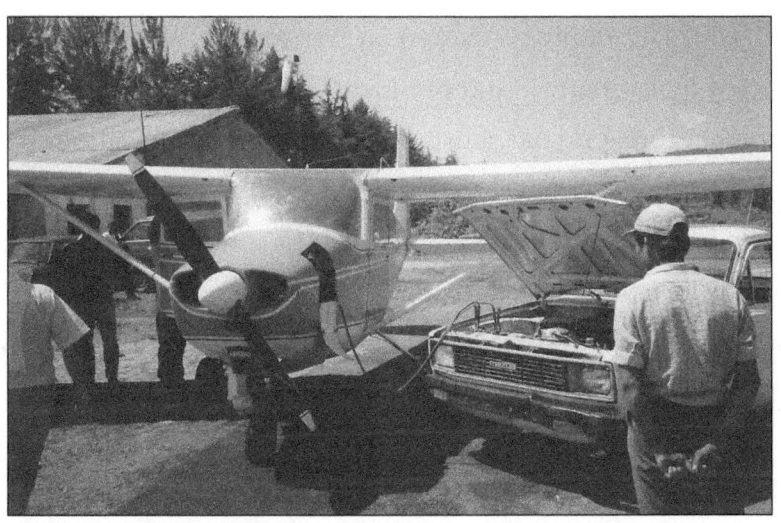

"Jumper cables were necessary to start the plane."

Chapter 5

PRAYER AND COURAGE

"I have come that they may have life, and that they may have it more abundantly." (John 10:10)

For many years I worked with "Forward Edge International," (F.E.I.), a ministry located in Vancouver, Washington and directed by its founder and president, Joseph Anfuso. Its thriving purpose was to send out short-term mission teams to various parts of the world. The teams brought the good news of Jesus Christ to people impacted by disaster and need. Joseph is a man God uses to bring people together to help those in need. Recently, F.E.I was called upon to administrate one of the largest teams they ever organized.

Albania

Joe suggested I go with Dave Booker, one of the F.E.I. team leaders, to help with a large youth team coming to Albania. Their project was to build a playground for an orphanage in Tirana, the capital of Albania. Several months before the team left, I spoke with Dave about helping him with the project. Dave agreed and we traveled together arriving two days early to prepare for the upcoming week.

All preparations were made by the time the team arrived from several different nations. It was the largest team I ever worked with: composed of more than sixty youth and thirty adults.

The youth on the team made quick friends with the children at the orphanage. Many of the men watched over the youth programs and games. I worked with the men on the playground construction project. Within five working days, the playground was completed and the children were having a great time on many of its functions. The favorite activity was a 200-foot-long Zip-Line. It consisted of a 200-foot cable attached to the top of a post supporting a treehouse which was twenty feet off the ground. The other end of the cable was attached to a post about six feet off the ground. A seat was attached, dangling down about 4 feet from the cable. The children would walk up a ramp to ride the Zip-Line from the tree house down to the post. A "stop" was put on the cable to prevent the seat and rider from slamming into the post. When it was completed, it became great fun for the youth and adults as well.

On the day before the team was to leave Albania, some youth from the team performed a biblical drama of Jesus Christ's crucifixion and resurrection. At the end of the drama, an invitation was given to receive Jesus Christ as Lord and Savior. Some were weeping while many came forward. It was the best project of the week.

If you confess with your mouth the Lord Jesus and believe in your heart that God has raised Him from the dead, you will be saved. (Romans 10:9)

The next day the team was eager to go home. Dave and I stayed on for an extra day with the same family who hosted us our first night in Albania. Dave was a joy to be with. He treated the host family to an enchilada dinner making a terrible mess in the kitchen, but all of us chipped in to help in the cleanup.

Early the next morning, Dave and I were at the Tirana airport preparing to return to the States. Our itinerary called for a one-night layover in Athens, Greece. With time to spare in Athens, we visited the ancient Acropolis, from where government officials once ruled the land. We rested that night and were on early flights back home the next morning.

After arriving in St. Louis, I shared my experiences in Albania with Barb. The work in Albania was a challenge as I had never worked with such a large team before. I considered it a blessing to know that God had provided me with sufficient grace to do such work. Little did I know, God had plans for me to work with F.E.I. for many years.

Back to Guatemala

After being home for a few weeks, I was asked to lead a seven-day evangelistic team coming from California going to Guatemala. Barb stayed home because of the short time the team would be there.

Prayer and Courage

On the morning of my travel to Guatemala, my daughter-in-law, Monica, and her sister-in-law, Staci, came running down the concourse to talk to me. Darin and Monica had prayed for a baby for a long time and were still waiting.

When Monica and Staci saw me, Staci said, "Mr. Kassebaum, please bring a baby back for Darin and Monica."

I thought, *Yeah, right! Where am I going to get a baby?*

We talked, laughed, and then I boarded the plane for Guatemala.

The righteous are as bold as a lion. (Proverbs 28:1)

When I arrived in Guatemala, my friends Quique and Carolina Cazali, with their two small daughters, Anita and Lilly, met me at the airport. They were now living in the Capitol City to assist in the pastoral work of one of the growing Verbo churches. Anita and Lilly watched as I unpacked my bags. When they saw two toy dolls I had brought for them, their eyes got big and smiles lit their faces.

After spending time with Quique and Carolina, I made plans for the upcoming week and then rested that night. By midafternoon on the following day, the team arrived at the airport and were transported to the small town of Chiquimulia. The team served as a medical-evangelistic outreach for several days.

At the end of the week, a brother from the team and I went into the city to get some Sunday clothes for me to preach in. When we arrived at Quique's house, the two little girls met us at the door, jabbering in Spanish. I understood the word, "Muñeca," meaning "Doll." I thought they were thanking me for giving them the two dolls when I first arrived. They ran to my bedroom pulling me along with their hands. There on the bed was what looked like another doll. The two little ones squeezed between me and the door to get into the room while laughing and jabbering. My friend went and picked up the doll on the bed and it moved.

I looked at Carolina and asked, "Whose baby is this?"

Carolina, a bit giggly, said, "This is your baby, Don."

"What do you mean, 'My Baby?' I asked, trying to understand what was happening!

Carolina laughed and said, "This is your baby for Darin and Monica."

"Where did you get this baby?" I asked, wondering what was going on.

Carolina answered, "We received this baby at the hospital this morning from a young girl who had just given birth but had no means to care for the child. Since she knew Quique and me well, she wanted us to help find the perfect home for her baby boy."

I immediately took the baby from my friend's arms. Tears welled up in my eyes knowing the joy this little one would bring to Darin and Monica. Carolina instructed me on how to feed the baby and the times he would need to be fed. I put my new little grandson on one bed and I laid down on the other. He cried each time I laid him on the spare bed. After thirty minutes of crying, I decided to put him next to me on my bed with a pillow between us. Immediately, he stopped crying. That night I cared for him as if he was my own.

I knew how much Darin and Monica wanted a child, but it just hadn't happened. Now, the Kassebaum family would forever rejoice, knowing what God had done.

I returned home after an exciting time with the team and an incredible experience with my new grandson. Since the day of little Jesse's birth, three more sons and one daughter have been entrusted to Darin and Monica by the hand of God through adoptions. After all the excitement, I felt I was now ready for any team that "Joe of F.E.I." would request me to lead.

Back to Albania

I was home for several months when I was asked by Joe to lead another team to Albania. Surprisingly, there was no project or plan for the team. Neither was there a church or other ministry in Albania connected to F.E.I. I knew the manager of, "The Stephan's Center," a restaurant where many pastors and missionaries spent time discussing plans for upcoming outreaches. So, I agreed to lead the team with Barb, leaving a couple of days early in hopes of developing a project for the team.

Upon arriving at the Tirana airport, we were greeted by Tom, the manager of the restaurant. Tom informed me he had a full day lined up for pastors to meet with me. I was thrilled as Tom drove us to the restaurant. We walked a few blocks to the home where I stayed on my first visit to Albania. Lilli, the owner of the home, was excited to hear we would stay with her again.

After speaking with several different pastors the next day, I met Memli and Landi, pastors of a Christian church in Albania.

They were interested in having our team work with their church during the upcoming week. I asked how our team could serve them suggesting projects like painting the church, their house or maybe doing some needed carpentry work and yard work.

The answer was no, no, and no.

"Well then, what would you like us to do?" I asked.

Memli paused for a moment and answered, "Come and teach us how to evangelize."

I had not done much evangelism, but I responded hesitantly, "Sure! When do you want us to come?"

Memli was quick to answer, "Tuesday evening at 6:30 p.m."

"Okay!" I agreed, thinking, *Well, we have three days to pray and prepare.*

The team arrived at the end of the week and listened as I shared with the six-team members what had transpired previously. Immediately, the team began to pray corporately. They were concerned about this objective and their purpose in Albania. There was no manual project for the team to do and not one of the team members felt like they were prepared to teach on how to evangelize.

I was invited to preach at their Saturday evening service. The meeting was held in a public theater building. When we arrived, I was introduced to a pretty, young girl who wore tight short, shorts. She was to be my translator during the service. I couldn't believe it and thought, *How am I to preach God's Word with her dressed like that on the platform with me?* I immediately began asking for God's help and intervention.

When the time came for me to preach, the two of us climbed the steps of the platform. I began to preach and as fast as my words came from my lips, she was translating them. It was as if I wasn't even there. She was wonderful. I never acknowledged there was someone translating for me. I paid no attention to her.

I can do all things through Christ who strengthens me. (Philippians 4:13)

However, I did notice a young man sitting in the back of the church shaking his head from side to side in disagreement on everything I spoke. It was very annoying and I thought to myself, *Why doesn't he just leave if he is in total disagreement with me.* I spoke on forgiveness from the life of Joseph. At the end of the message, I gave an invitation for people to come for prayer who desired to forgive someone in their life. The young man came running to the front to be first to receive God's help. I could hardly believe it. After I had prayed for the young man, the man appeared so grateful to God for releasing him of his burden. It made no sense to me what had happened.

Later that evening, while telling this story to the pastor of the church, the pastor laughed and told me that in the Albanian language a "Yes" is shaking your head from side to side and a "No" was shaking your head up and down. Now it made sense. This brother was in agreement with my message from the beginning.

The next morning, the team was invited to go to a church service in "Iba," a village, about forty minutes up in the mountains outside of Tirana. I was again invited to preach. Upon arriving, I discovered no one had shown up for the meeting except for three children. It seems there was a wedding being celebrated in the village and all the village townspeople were at the wedding. So, the whole team decided to join the wedding. We were fed a lot of food, given a pack of cigarettes, a bottle of whiskey, and instructed to dance with the bride's family. I thought dancing was going just a bit too far and told Pastor Memli that I just couldn't do the dancing bit.

The pastor said, "Do you see that man over there with the bulgy black pocket in his trousers? Well, that's the bride's father and he wants you to dance with his daughter. By the way, that bulge in his trousers is his gun."

I responded quickly, "I'll dance, no problem, I'll dance."

Upon leaving late in the day, we were given more cigarettes. It was an experience no one would forget.

For the next two days, the team rose by 6:00 a.m. for prayer followed by breakfast. Each day I suggested we go out in pairs, walking and praying in the streets of Albania. After lunch, we spent time together in the Word. One of the team members would share revelation they were receiving through the Word. We would then pair up again to walk and pray.

He called the twelve to Himself, and began to send them out two by two, and gave them power over unclean spirits. (Mark 6:7)

By the end of the second day of walking the streets of Tirana, spending much time in prayer, reading God's Word, and taking authority over spiritual darkness, we felt the presence and closeness of God. By the time evening came on their third day, the team gathered at the pastor's house for a meeting. I shared a word on evangelism as the meeting was about to end. I asked the church if there was anything else the team could do for them.

Immediately, Pastor Memli said, "Yes, come again tomorrow night and teach us how to use the word you taught us on tonight. We will all break up into small groups and each one of you on the team will lead a small group in evangelism."

Without thinking, I responded, "Sure, we'll be glad to do that, right team?"

Then I thought, *I think they all want to lay hands on me, that is, around my throat.*

Wednesday came and again the team spent much time in prayer and sharing scriptures. Each one was crying out for the Holy Spirit to move through the evangelistic outreach that night and bring many to Jesus. By 6:30 p.m., the team was at the pastor's house to meet with people from the church. They spent about thirty minutes praying together and then broke up into five separate groups. The plan was for each group to go in a different direction in that city. Though they all had spent time in prayer and had at least one team member with them, some church people were feeling apprehensive about the outreach. A few had never knocked on doors or done anything in the town square or used a drama to reach people, but time was passing and the moment of evangelism had arrived.

Pastor Memli spoke up and said, "I want to go with Don and Barb. I want to see how this is done."

I thought, *Oh, great, why couldn't I have gotten one of the new believers.*

We all took off walking towards an apartment complex. Arriving there, Pastor Memli knocked on one door while Barb knocked on another. Suddenly, both doors opened and Memli began talking to both families at the same time. Confusion resulted. Memli, kindly excused himself from the door he had knocked on and came to Barb's rescue. Barb and the group were all invited inside and listened to the family story related by the lady of the house. There was a separation in her marriage. Barb shared her personal testimony with her. Though Barb never experienced divorce or separation, she did experience a very worldly lifestyle before giving her heart to Jesus. After about twenty minutes of sharing, Barb asked her if she would like to give her life to Jesus.

The woman said, "Oh, yes."

Barb had the privilege of leading this young woman to the Lord; a new daughter for Christ Jesus.

On our way back to Memli's house, I had the privilege of speaking to a drunk about Jesus. I remembered Chepi, also a drunk from San Pedro Pinula, Guatemala and the night he received Jesus into his life. Faith took hold and I talked to this man in a very simple way about Jesus. Then I asked this man if he wanted to have Jesus in his life.

The man said, "Yes."

So, I explained how this could be and then prayed with him to receive Jesus Christ right there on that street in Tirana. The people from the church were overwhelmed by the Lord. They all began rejoicing on their way back to Memli's house.

With the heart one believes unto righteousness, and with the mouth confession is made unto salvation. (Romans 10:10)

Upon arriving at Memli's house, I saw the man who was drunk just a short time before. He was at Memli's house wanting to hear more about Jesus. The next day, I saw him again on the streets of Tirana. He began asking me and another team member about our faith in Christ Jesus. We found someone to translate for us and began talking to him about his new faith in the God of all creation. After listening intently, he was given an invitation to come to the next church meeting and be introduced to other Christians.

Evangelism meant so much more to me now that I was able to see sinners coming to Christ. For the next several days, we found ourselves in a new place with God. We climbed high on a mountainside overlooking the village of Iba. We prayed for the people of Iba to know Jesus and for the whole village to receive Him as their Lord and Savior. We prayed for the church in Iba and for Pastor Memli, Luiza, and the other leaders with them. We prayed for the whole community of believers to unite together and overcome the darkness in this place where God was shedding His light. Then we all went back down into the village and shared God's Word with many children before we returned to Tirana.

The next day, we went to the place where it is believed Paul and Silas spent time preaching God's Word. The team members then returned to their host houses to share their goodbyes with their host family and prepare for their long flights back to the States.

We came home excited in what God had done through the team in Albania. The past two weeks were incredible times. For the first time in our lives, we spent whole days in prayer and the Word while seeking God for the days that followed. Walking each day through the city of Tirana, two by two, was an experience in itself. Listening to the revelations that other team members were receiving was a new blessing. Finding grace for each person on the team and from the church was an extraordinary gift from God I had never seen before. I received so much more from God and God's people than what I gave. It all centered around prayer. God was with us and still is.

At home I woke up at one or two in the morning being wide-awake because of jet lag. I thought, *What a blessing this is. I'm not going to waste this time when I can't sleep. I'll get up and pray until I get sleepy.* The jet lag continued for several weeks and I hoped it would never stop.

If anyone is in Christ, he is a new creation; old things have passed away; behold, all things have become new. (2 Corinthians 5:17)

A Guatemalan Orphanage

After several weeks of being home, Barb and I were called to lead another team of nine people from our home church to Guatemala.

Prayer and Courage

Our project was to rebuild a rotted-out mobile home where orphan children could live safely. The mobile home was almost a total disaster. The floor was filled with big holes. Some of the walls also had huge holes in them. In the bathroom, you could see through to the outside. The men and some women from the team spent time putting new plywood and tile down for flooring and new paneling on the walls. Some of the ladies made curtains for the windows. New plumbing was installed, and by the end of the week, the home was ready for occupancy. This all took place in six working days. By the time the work was finished, our team had made this mobile home look like a doll house.

The team began each day with an hour of prayer, praise, worship, and the Word. Each day a different team member would bring a teaching from God's Word. Breakfast would then be served and the work would begin. At the end of the week the team gathered together for one last meeting, which was conducted on the site of the orphanage where all the work had originated. The evening began with a time of prayer and worship. I shared a passage of scripture with the team from Joshua 4:1-7. It was the testimony of Joshua crossing the Jordan as they were going into the Promised Land with the twelve tribes of Israel. One man from each tribe set in place on dry ground a rock to commemorate the crossing of the Jordan at flood stage. These stones were set in place so that in future years when their children would ask why those stones were set in place here, they would be reminded how God dried up the river Jordan for all the people of Israel to walk through.

In response, each team member went out and brought back a rock from the property to set up a monument that would be a memorial for our team. The Holy Spirit was touching the hearts of the team members as I saw tears in their eyes. It was a time of Holy Spirit encounter. He was preparing our hearts for our departure from Guatemala in the morning.

Early the next morning, the team members said their goodbyes. There were tears in some of their eyes as they boarded their flights and were off to their homes in the States.

Kobe, Japan

Shortly after Barb and I arrived home, a devastating earthquake struck Kobe, Japan. I was asked to travel there with another man from California to assess the damage and to consider if F.E.I. could be of help in the restoration process. After travel preparations were made, I was on my way. Shortly after arriving in Kobe, I learned quickly there wasn't much of a Holy Spirit movement in the country. At that time, it was statistically reported that a large church had around seventy-five members. The church that I was sent to had twelve members and ten of them were women. The pastor had been working for many years to raise this church up. He, his wife, and the members of his church were very kind to me. The church building was destroyed and needed men with knowledge on how to rebuild it. Its structure was leaning to one side and too dangerous even to enter.

After I returned home and spoke with the leaders of F.E.I., they felt that it would be unwise to send teams of inexperienced men and women to reconstruct this building or even to tear down the existing building and build a new one. I had a close friend, Daniel Culley, who was qualified and possibly able to spend an ongoing length of time in Japan to oversee the project. I thought there was a good possibility he might want to be involved.

So, I met with Daniel. After thinking about it and seeking God's direction, Daniel believed God was in it for him. It wasn't long before his bags were packed and he was off to Japan. He was the force that pulled it all together. The existing church building was taken down and a new building was constructed in its place. The Lord was in this project from the beginning. He used Daniel as His blessing to the church.

Barb and I evaluated our lives and work over the past twelve months. We realized all we learned about ministry while in Albania was the key to all the other work God had led us through. This assessment showed us that our relationship with God was the key to the victory in what we believed God was doing through our lives. We saw that more was accomplished through our lives in four days of prayer in Albania than in all the twenty-seven other days in the month. The ministry was changing and a new season was dawning.

Seek first the kingdom of God and his righteousness, and all these things shall be added to you. (Matthew 6:33)

"The final project (zip line) with team members and children from the orphanage in Albania."

Chapter 6

JOURNEYS OF ENLIGHTENMENT

I heard the voice of the Lord saying, "Whom shall I send? And who will go for us?" And I said, "Here am I. Send me!" (Isaiah 6:8) *NIV*

We were living life in anticipation of what lay ahead. Barb and I had incredible new experiences in Guatemala and Albania and now God was calling us into a new territory. We weren't exactly sure how God would use us, but we were certain God was sending us. We would travel further south into the Americas to preach the gospel and observe how F.E.I. could be a helping hand to God's people. We would also begin the work of sending aid to the poor and needy in Guatemala.

El Salvador

A few days into the new year, we boarded a plane in St. Louis, Missouri for our first stop, El Salvador. We were to meet up with Remberto Lazo, the pastor of a growing Verbo church in San

Salvador, the nation's capitol. I was invited to speak in a leadership meeting at the church the first evening of our arrival.

We arrived at the airport in San Salvador and were taken to the church by one of its members. A doctor, Rafa Morales, who was fluent in English and just starting his new career in the medical field, came to meet us.

A man's heart plans his way, but the Lord directs his steps. (Proverbs 16:9)

Rafa shared with us how he and Sarita, his wife, had just completed their doctorate studies. They were now both looking forward to their new careers. As I listened to Rafa, a desire rose up in me to invite him and his wife to the U.S. and be part of the Covenant Discipleship Training (CDT) program. The program would help prepare them to live a life of discipleship in the medical field. I explained to Rafa about the nine-month CDT course in St. Louis, Missouri.

The next day Rafa contacted me asking me to meet with his pastor, Remberto, to share about the CDT program. We all met later that day. Remberto felt an excitement for Rafa and Sarita. After sharing it with Remberto, I knew the rest was up to Rafa, Sarita, and the Lord. I gave him all the enrollment information, U.S. telephone numbers, and people to contact. Seeing Rafa's excitement, I became more enthusiastic about the purpose of our travel to El Salvador.

The following day, Barb and I met Moises Navarrete and his wife Helen. They were raising up another Verbo church just south of the capital city. Moises was a vibrant, emotional, and exciting pastor who was leading his church with the most exuberant praise and worship that we had ever encountered. They jumped, danced, and ran around the building, praising the Lord with all their hearts. It was an inspiring sight to behold.

Before leaving El Salvador, Barb and I met with Remberto one more time. He had a few more questions for me about the CDT program. By mid-day, we were off to Managua, Nicaragua.

Nicaragua

After landing in Managua, we met with Bob Trolese, a wonderful missionary pastor from the U.S. who was raising up a growing Verbo church in Managua. I discovered that the church in Managua had sent out men with their families to raise up two other churches in Nicaragua's coastal regions. Bob wanted us to visit these churches, so he hired a small plane to transport us to Bluefields for two days and then to Puerto Las Cabezas for an additional two days.

Landing on a grassy field in Bluefields, Barb and I met the pastor of the Verbo church, Ed Jazentschke, his wife Lijia, and their three children. Ed was a delight to talk to. It was easy to see that Ed and Lijia were a team. When they spoke, they spoke with confidence that God was with them and that He was using them both to bring the Kingdom of God into the lives of the people in Bluefields. We didn't want to leave. Ed and Lijia appeared to be true disciples of Bob Trolese.

We rested well in Ed and Lijia's home. Their hospitality made us feel like we were part of what God was doing in Bluefields, even though we had just met. When it was time to leave, we felt like we were leaving friends from long ago.

We climbed aboard the aircraft and were on our way to Puerto Las Cabezas to meet with Earl Bowie and his wife Alicia. We arrived late in the day and once again our small plane landed on a grassy field. Earl and Alicia were so kind to us. Listening to them, they sounded as if they had no needs whatsoever. Yet, when we entered their home we were warned about where to walk on the rotting floor. The floor was so bad, if we didn't put our foot on a floor joist, we could possibly fall through to the under part of the house. There were huge holes in the floor where it appeared someone had stepped in the wrong place. There were many people there that day to serve in any way they could. It appeared to be something like community living. Everyone seemed happy.

This poor man cried out, and the Lord heard him, and saved him out of all his troubles. (Psalm 34:6)

Earl, as poor as he was, insisted we sleep in he and his wife's bed that night. This was our first experience sleeping under a mosquito net. The next day Earl showed us around the community; opening our eyes to its many needs. He spoke about the church wanting to have a school, a medical clinic, and other facilities to help the poor and needy in that village. It was quite evident Earl had a vision on how to bring God's Kingdom into Puerto Las Cabezas.

After being with Ed and Lijia and then Earl and Alicia, we were pleased to see the dedication these couples had to God and

His people by raising up these churches in these two small villages. Earl and Alicia appeared to be living in near poverty, yet, never complained about their situation.

Barb and I were serving God by just visiting these areas. We saw a level of poverty we never knew existed. They needed lumber for their houses and property for a church building along with a steady income of financial support to continue to live and do God's work.

We were so grateful to God for the opportunity to go and experience the needs. It brought a new perspective of life to us as we returned to Managua. Meeting Bob Trolese a second time was a privilege given by God. He wanted to hear about Ed and Lijia and Earl and Alicia. It was a privilege to bring back a positive report. I told Bob though I saw much physical poverty, I saw no spiritual poverty. I assured Bob I would take a good report to Joseph Anfuso at F.E.I.

Ecuador

By the end of the week, our time with Bob came to a close. We left Nicaragua en route to Quito, Ecuador. When the plane set down in Quito, Jim DeGolyer was there to take us to his home. Jim was one of the founders of the Verbo work in Ecuador. He was a man who was never afraid of the impossible. He took on any task that he knew God had assigned to him.

There were three large Verbo churches in Quito. I was asked to preach in both services in one of them that upcoming Sunday morning. God's presence was upon His people that morning and I saw a great movement of the Holy Spirit at the end of each service.

The last couple I prayed with asked for more of God. They wanted to know Him intimately. Seeing people like this was special to us. I thought, *Oh, that we all could have that deep desire for more of Him and less of us.*

He must become greater; I must become less.
(John 3:30 NIV)

The following day, we relaxed, free of any agenda. We enjoyed being with Jim and his wife, Mary. They were a gracious couple who spent nearly their whole married life as missionaries in Guatemala and Ecuador.

Jim and Mary took us on a little site-seeing tour of Quito and then to an orphanage for handicapped children. Members of their church oversaw this work at the orphanage and were filled with God's grace for this most extraordinary ministry. We then visited another church outreach that Jim and Mary helped raise up. It was a ministry towards teenage boys, who had at one time, lived on the streets of Quito. Through the Verbo ministries, they were given an apartment to live in and opportunities to learn a trade or have further education. It was easy to see how grateful Jim and Mary were to God for opening these doors of opportunity through hard work and trusting God.

The next day, our tour continued as we journeyed through the mountains of Ecuador. By midafternoon, we arrived in Pasaje and met up with the brothers from the Verbo church. I went with some of the men from the church to view a plot of land that was recently given to them to erect a Christian school. While there, I received a word from God for the church. It was out of the book of Numbers, chapter thirteen. I thought I was to give this word to the men I traveled with, but while they were standing together in a circle praying, the opportunity for me to speak never came. The prayer circle disbanded and each man went his own way.

I was asked to preach that night and felt honored knowing the confidence the brothers had in me. I remembered God's Word from the book of Numbers given to me while standing on that donated land that afternoon. I began reading, meditating, and praying for God to show me how to use this scripture.

As the meeting got underway, I stepped outside, into a small corridor to pray for a brother. Suddenly, the Holy Spirit came upon me and I nearly fell down. Bent over and leaning against a concrete wall, I received all that God's Holy Spirit was giving me. By the time I was to preach, I was filled with God's presence. God's Word came to me with power and authority. Soon, the front of the platform was filled with people calling out for more of God. My heart was stirred as I witnessed God moving among His people.

In all your ways acknowledge Him, And He shall direct your paths. (Proverbs 3:6)

The next morning the people of the church blessed us through their hospitality. It wasn't easy to leave them, but now it was time to visit the church in Santa Lucia.

Jim drove through the mountains towards the small village of Santa Lucia. There we met another Verbo church pastor and his wife. They were so happy to be serving the Lord and to see Jim and Mary. They lived in a small home high up in the mountains with no running water or electricity in a very cold climate. Every day, a dense cloud would cover their village. They had devised a system to collect water from the cloud. The cloud was critical to watering their crops. After spending a couple of hours there, we left for Cuenca continuing our journey through the mountains. Arriving late in the day, we received a hearty welcome from the brothers of Cuenca's Verbo church.

The next day there were no meetings to attend. The brothers only wanted us to meet some of the leaders of the church. The congregation was made up of many medical doctors and nurses. Some of the doctors took Barb and me to a building that God had blessed them with. It was being renovated to be used as a hospital. They had also received another building that was to be used as a medical clinic. It was easy to see the testimony of God's goodness in their church. Later that day, Jim, Mary, Barb, and I flew back to Quito where I would be preaching the next day in another one of the three churches.

After the Sunday service, we returned to Jim and Mary's house to prepare for our departure back to the states the next morning. The previous two week activities revealed its purpose for many. Rafa and Sarita from El Salvador would come to the U.S. for discipleship training. The people of Ecuador showed a desire to have more of God in their lives. We saw how God was using us in these two nations. We became more excited about God's ongoing plan of sending aid to the poor in Guatemala.

Pursuing the Vision

After we arrived home, memories of God's call returned to us. It had been a little more than a year since God had put a new vision in our hearts to send a convoy of trucks filled with physical aid to the poor in Guatemala. By God's leading, we were ready to pursue that vision. We began by collecting and preparing the aid for shipment. After many months of preparation, it was now time to ship our first container.

I contacted Ronny Gilmore, whom I had met on my first missionary trip to Guatemala. I asked him to come and help us load our first container. Ronny, through his many years of living and working in Guatemala, gave great advice concerning loading and shipping this first container.

Greater love has no one than this, than to lay down one's life for his friends. (John 15:13)

It was a very cold Saturday morning in O'Fallon, Missouri, when men and women arrived at our warehouse to help load the huge container. It was originally thought to be forty-foot long, but when it arrived, we found it was a fifty-five-foot container. It was a special blessing from God. My only concern was whether we had enough aid to fill that huge box. I had no idea what God's plan was for that day.

In the warehouse that morning, I was feeling the failure of not having a convoy of trucks. I had one long fifty-five-foot trailer, but not much to put in it. Then God showed up.

As I was standing on the warehouse dock with the door of the trailer open, I saw a parade of pickup trucks, trailers, farm trucks, and automobiles coming around the corner of the building loaded with items of aid.

I heard God say, "Here is your convoy of trucks, loaded with aid."

I wept and gave thanks to God for His faithfulness and thought, *"Who can compare with our God?"*

To whom then will you liken God? Or what likeness will you compare to Him? (Isaiah 40:18)

By 8:00 a.m., the work of loading the container had begun. More than twenty people had come out to help load. Some were taking inventory of every item being loaded. Some were sorting clothes, toys, and small items. Others were packing the sorted items and still others were keeping the hot chocolate and coffee flowing. Everyone had a special function to perform. By 3:00 p.m., the container was three-fourths full and we were running out of aid items.

Then two pickups and a large automobile from Cahokia, Illinois arrived. They were filled with more aid for the needy in Guatemala. With all that was in the two pickups and the automobile, the container was nearly full. As dusk was setting, a large van entered the scene loaded with computers that I felt were sent from heaven. With the extra aid from Cahokia and the computers, only one large box was needed to completely fill the container. It just so happened there was one large empty box sitting on the blacktop driveway that read, "FRAGILE – TV." It was the perfect size to fit into the vacant hole to completely fill the huge container and prevent the cargo from shifting around.

It was after 5:30 p.m. when in the dark using headlights to give light to load the last few items plus the empty TV box, the doors were closed and locked. Everyone screamed and clapped their hands to acknowledge what God had done. Then we all ran into the warehouse for hot drinks.

While in the warehouse, warming up, Lou and Denise from Cahokia asked me if Barb and I were planning to travel to Guatemala soon. If so would we allow them to follow us through Mexico to Guatemala. We were delighted to hear their request yet were somewhat cautious. We all agreed to discuss this possibility at a later time. Within a couple of days, we had agreed to permit our new friends to travel with us.

In less than a week, we met our new friends, Lou and Denise on the highway going west to Springfield, Missouri. Both vehicles were meeting up with the third vehicle in Springfield. Arriving on time, John and Lisa were in their pickup with a camper shell waiting for us and our Cahokia friends. We three couples were soon on our way.

At the beginning of the week, Barb and I had put together a set of rules each family agreed to follow for the safety of everyone:

a. No extra medical supplies, instruments or pharmaceuticals would be allowed.

b. No extra food, tires, mechanical parts, firearms, liquor, or any items that could potentially cause problems crossing the Mexican or Guatemalan borders.
c. The three vehicles will travel close together at all times.
d. If one car faltered, the other two vehicles must wait with him.
e. Much caution will be taken with personal and vehicle paperwork.
f. No arguments with any government officials.
g. No night driving except in a total emergency.

By midmorning, all three vehicles left Missouri and entered Oklahoma and then headed south toward Texas. The threesome passed through Dallas without difficulty around 4:00 p.m. and stopped to refuel and eat dinner. While at the table, I learned that John had a freezer full of meat and frozen food in the back of his pickup. I was furious! John had broken one of the rules we had all agreed to abide by. In addition, I found out about mechanical parts, tires, medical supplies, medical instruments, and pharmaceuticals that were also in their truck. I didn't know what to say or do. I didn't want to abandon them to their own ways, but what was I to do? Discussing it with Barb, we decided to pray and ask for God's wisdom.

I was concerned about the extra items John and Lisa brought, plus the weather began getting windy and bitterly cold. On top of this, our scout began to run poorly. We all agreed to stop at the next rest area and spend the night there in our vehicles.

I will be strong and my heart will take courage.
(Psalm 27:14 ESV)

Early the next morning, my concerns grew about the scout running poorly. John was driving an older pickup truck and seemed to know much about mechanics. I talked to him about the problem and he helped me fix the scout with a new gas-line filter. Then we were off and running again.

Before we left home, I had reserved three rooms at a Christian retreat center near San Antonio, TX close to the border of Mexico to rest for the night. Arriving there at 5:00 p.m., John and Lisa asked me for forgiveness and agreed to leave all the food and medical supplies at the Christian retreat center. They agreed to follow all the rules that we had set forth from the beginning. I thanked them and was filled with peace about the outcome.

Early in the morning, the prompting of the Holy Spirit awakened me. I heard God tell me to take all the food, mechanical parts, and medical supplies with us through Mexico. What a surprise this was! I was excited. When 6:00 a.m. came, I told John and the whole group what God had spoken to me in the middle of the night. Everyone was filled with joy. Within a short time, the vehicles were reloaded and we left to cross the border.

Entering Mexico, all three vehicles were immediately directed to stop at the custom and immigration offices. We parked next to each other in a specified parking lot for customs inspections. Soon the inspecting officers came and asked for all three vehicles to be unloaded. Everything we were carrying was to be removed. We placed all the medical supplies, syringes, and equipment, plus food, mechanical tools, and parts on the tables provided.

We all stood by watching the inspection-process and praying quietly that God would have the inspecting officers approve everything for transport. The officers climbed up into the back of the pickup to inspect the freezer full of frozen meat and other food. In a short time, we were told to reload everything, fill out the paperwork, and be on our way. We headed south once again giving thanks to God.

We drove for about an hour south of the border and were detained at another checkpoint. Once again we were asked to unload everything for inspection. As we began unloading the vehicles, the officers saw how inconvenient and difficult it was to do. The officers stopped us from unloading, told us to reload it all, and be on our way. We praised God once again for His favor.

On the last day traveling through Mexico, we arrived at the southern border immigration office. We turned in our paperwork, but when John finished turning in his, he walked away from the counter leaving his passport laying on it. When I saw what John had done, I picked up the passport, took it to him, and spoke strongly to never let that happen again. John felt bad and asked for forgiveness. I appreciated John's attitude and responded graciously.

After all the paperwork was completed, we drove for about fifteen minutes to the Guatemalan border. I was the first to go through customs and immigration. After about twenty minutes, Barb and I were approved to enter Guatemala. I picked up our paperwork and went out to the car to wait for the other two brothers and their families. Sitting in my vehicle, I searched for my passport for nearly ten minutes, but could not find it. I saw John and Lisa sitting in their pickup, waiting for Lou, Denise, and their children. I hated to tell John that I'd lost my passport, but I didn't know what else to do. I went to John's truck and told him my problem.

John showed no sympathy, but then Lisa started laughing and told John to give me my passport. I had left it on the officer's desk in the immigration office. By now they were both laughing. I just thanked him kindly.

Let patience have its perfect work, that you may be perfect and complete, lacking nothing. (James 1:4)

Our travel through Mexico over the previous four days went well and we were approved to travel on into Guatemala. Barb and I said goodbye and left the convoy to travel the six-hour journey to Guatemala City. John and Lou, with their wives and family, drove seven hours more through the mountainous regions of Guatemala to reach their destination.

Four days after Barb and I arrived in the Capitol City of Guatemala, we were notified our container was in the port of Puerto Barrios. The container would be released from the port when the taxes on the cargo were paid. The taxes were more than I had anticipated. As I searched for a solution, I found that each foreign passport would allow a fixed amount of cargo value to enter Guatemala free of taxes. With twelve foreign passports, I would be able to bring all the cargo on the container into Guatemala free of charge. I hired a small engine prop plane and flew up into the mountains to retrieve passports from our missionary friends who traveled with us through Mexico the previous week. I was able to acquire fifteen passports. It seemed every missionary wanted to get in on the action of getting aid to the needy people of Guatemala. Soon, I was on my way back to the Capitol City with more than enough passports to begin the distribution of aid.

Next, I was told that the container needed to be inspected. As they began opening the doors to inspect the cargo, the box that read: "FRAGILE – TV" came tumbling out of the container. Everyone scattered and then laughed after discovering the box was empty. With that bit of excitement, the inspecting officers approved the contents of the container.

The container was then taken to a warehouse donated by "Feed the Children." The aid was unloaded and divided up among fifteen churches we were working with at the time. After receiving the aid in one of the churches in a village near the coast, an F.E.I. team helped distribute the aid. A lot of clothes, shoes, toys, and miscellaneous household items were given away. One family received a mattress for a double bed and carried it up a steep incline for more than an hour since no vehicle or road went to their small village. The following Sunday, that same F.E.I. team worshiped in their beautiful church. From what we saw and experienced, the container of aid was a real blessing to the needy in Guatemala. It was a new undertaking for us, but it was only the beginning.

Journeys of Enlightenment

"Photo of convoy of trucks."

"Overview of all the aid to be loaded on container."

"Don and volunteers unloading container in Guatemala."

Chapter 7
STRESSED BUT BLESSED!

Trust in the LORD, and do good; Dwell in the land, and feed on His faithfulness. (Psalm 37:3)

Sending aid to the poor in other nations was also the beginning for our evangelism ministry, but we never gave a thought to the financial responsibilities of this new ministry. The pet shampoo business, under the leadership of our sons, was growing and the income we received from this business supported our expenses while in the U.S. However, it was not enough to meet all our needs when we traveled to other countries. With the additional cost of collecting and shipping aid in forty-foot containers, we needed to raise more funds.

Barb and I solicited work to build decks and paint houses. New opportunities started to flow in. We were kept busy and the profit was growing. One hundred percent of the profit was put into a charitable fund to be used specifically to help the poor in other nations. God blessed our work. I enjoyed the carpentry and Barb assisted me as needed. This endeavor continued for several years.

He who sows sparingly will also reap sparingly, and he who sows bountifully will also reap bountifully.
(2 Corinthians 9:6)

One hot July day, while I was working on a proposal to build a deck for a prospective client, I received a call from Joe LoMonaco, a brother from Anchorage, Alaska. He contacted me to inquire about a specific ministry to children in San Pedro La Laguna, Guatemala, and wanted to verify it. I knew nothing of the ministry, but we were to leave for Guatemala soon, so I told Joe I would make it a point to inquire about the children's ministry during our next trip.

A few weeks later, we flew to Guatemala. We spent our time teaching and preaching among the churches we had relationships with. Three days before we were to leave Guatemala, I remembered my commitment to Joe. So, we drove to Panajachel, a tourist town on beautiful Lake Atitlan. From Panajachel, it was an hour and a half crossing the lake on a ferry. Upon arrival in San Pedro La Laguna, we inquired about a ministry to children located in the lake town. Led by children, we were escorted to the home of Pastor Emilio and Esther Batz.

After we introduced ourselves, we sat and listened to Emilio and Esther share their vision of a Christian school on their property. They showed us some concrete footings that had been poured. Then we returned to the house to listen to more about Emilio and Esther's dream. I asked them when construction would begin on the walls.

Emilio replied, "As soon as we raise the money for the block, cement, and steel."

As Emilio spoke, I saw tears in his eyes. I asked Emilio what the materials would cost. Emilio said he thought about five thousand dollars. I remembered we had exactly five thousand dollars in our charitable fund. I offered to give that money to Emilio and Esther. As I wrote the check to their school fund, Emilio and Esther wept. They then gave prayers of thanksgiving to God for His provision. We left the couple excited to know that God had used us again for His purpose and glory.

The next day we boarded our flight back to the states. As the aircraft took off, I remembered I had committed to pay for three containers of aid costing $5,200 each within the next thirty days. I thought, *What have I done? I gave all the money that we had away. Where am I going to get more money to ship three containers of aid to Guatemala by the end of the month?* I began to weep as I thought, *I had enough money to pay for one of the three containers. Now I have nothing.*

I prayed and God encouraged me by reminding me He supplied the physical aid to fill the three containers. Then God asked me, "Am I not able to supply the money to pay for its transport to Guatemala?" My faith grew knowing God was indeed able.

He who supplies seed to the sower and bread for food will also supply and increase your store of seed and will enlarge the harvest of your righteousness. (2 Corinthians 9:10 NIV)

God Is Indeed Able

A little more than three weeks later, Barb and I were on our way to Groom Expo, a yearly pet grooming conference in Hershey, Pennsylvania. It was established and administrated by two Christian women, Sally Liddick and Gwen Shelly. They and their staff became close friends with us.

A short distance from Hershey is a Mennonite church where Barb and I had developed a great relationship with a precious family, Lamar and Mary Howe. Their whole church got involved in collecting aid to give to the needy in Guatemala. The day before the conference began, we went to see them and discovered Lamar had collected enough to fill more than two containers.

Lamar asked me the cost to send each container, I told him five thousand two hundred dollars.

Lamar then asked, "How many containers will you be sending?"

I took a deep breath and said, "Three."

Lamar seemed very inquisitive and asked, "Do you have the money to pay for all three containers?"

I didn't want to answer that question, but I said, "No, I don't."

Lamar asked, "How much do you have?"

I knew this question was coming and said, "Nothing!"

Lamar immediately responded, "Then how will you be able to send the containers out?"

By this time, I was tired of answering questions, but responded with all the grace I could muster, "I don't know, but since God supplied us with all this physical aid for Guatemala, He will supply all we need to transport the containers."

Lamar just laughed and stopped asking questions. After visiting for a short while longer, Barb and I returned to the conference center in Hershey.

Trust in the LORD with all your heart and lean not on your own understanding. (Proverbs 3:5)

We were given a booth at the conference to sell Guatemalan typicals which are items made by the Indians such as clothing, purses, toys, etc. We didn't sell much, but God blessed us in other ways.

Each year, a prayer breakfast was held on Sunday morning. Usually, there was someone who sang praise and worship songs and then someone shared a testimony of how God brought them through difficult times.

Without Barb and I knowing anything about it, Sally went up front and read a letter in front of five hundred participants that I had recently written to her. In the letter, I explained the work Barb and I were doing in Guatemala. I didn't ask for money or anything of monetary value. I only wanted Sally and Gwen to know about our work. After reading the letter, Sally asked us to come up front and share a few minutes concerning our work in Guatemala.

Barb talked about the Indian clothes she was wearing and how she had received them. When I began to talk, I couldn't hold back the tears of love I had for the Guatemalan people. After about ten minutes, we went and sat down at the table with our sons. Sally took the microphone, and with choked words, committed ten thousand dollars to our ministry. She invited others to also bless our work. I couldn't believe what was happening.

After breakfast, many people gave us donations for our work in Guatemala. I felt so blessed, I had a difficult time responding to the donors. When the conference ended that night, we had received more than twelve thousand dollars in donations.

We returned to Lamar's family and stayed with them until the two, forty-foot containers arrived. They were so kind to us. Lamar blessed me with a bowl of vanilla ice cream smothered with freshly picked strawberries. It was the tastiest dessert I had ever enjoyed at eleven o'clock at night. Lamar had more good news. He had told the elders of the church about our project. The elders agreed to commit five thousand five hundred dollars for shipping one of the containers. I was beside myself giving praise, glory, and honor to God. Our ministry received more than $17,500 that weekend in Hershey. We had more than enough to ship all three containers.

Two containers of aid from Pennsylvania and the one from our Missouri warehouse were loaded and shipped to Guatemala. We flew to Guatemala to ensure the containers were released from the port. Ronny Gilmore, my missionary friend, came to help with processing the containers.

Only after all paperwork was completed were the containers released from the port. Ronny and I looked for a warehouse to use in unloading the containers. Ronny had a friend who owned a hangar at the airport that was not being used. He donated it to Ronny for three days to unload the containers. This was a great blessing son was voted King of the high school homecoming. It was an exciting night for me and the whole Chism family.

The next day, I met Richard Nuti, an elder in the church who became my good friend. Richard was the administrator of the container project. He and several other men got into that hot container and started tightly packing everything. The men from the rehabilitation center wore their black and white striped clothes as they readily helped. It seemed that everyone was having fun working on the project together. By the end of the day, the container was full, the doors were closed, and the lock was put in place. The container was soon on its way to Guatemala.

The next morning, I preached at the church and later was invited to go for a ride in a small plane. It sounded like fun, so I went and then rested that evening before leaving for St. Louis in the morning.

Mom

Arriving home, I was told my mother was in the hospital. I visited her frequently and it appeared she was gaining strength and on her way to recovery. Mom was in her late seventies. She was tiny in size, but she had the power of a lion. While mom was in the hospital, one of my friends got married. We enjoyed the wedding and then I planned to visit mom later that day.

After the wedding, our friends from England, Ted and Esther Kent, came to stay with Barb and I. Ted asked if he could go to the hospital to visit mom with me. On the way to the hospital, I asked Ted to not talk about God to my mom. She was a devout Catholic and wanted to hear nothing about any other belief.

from God. If we had not found the warehouse, we would have been charged seventy-five dollars storage fee a day per container.

The containers were emptied and the church members came to the airplane hangar to receive the aid. The churches were so grateful for the work we were doing and thanked us over and over.

After the weekend, we were back at the airport boarding our flight back home. Somehow the flight attendant received a notice that we had been freely upgraded to first-class seating. We smiled at each other and accepted another blessing from God.

The blessing of the LORD makes one rich, and He adds no sorrow with it. (Proverbs 10:22)

Six weeks later, I left St. Louis, Missouri for Yerington, Nevada. Pastor Tom Chism of the Vineyard Church in Yerington, NV had contacted me through the F.E.I. office. He spoke with me about sending a container of aid to Guatemala. I was excited because I knew God was orchestrating this whole new relationship. I was to administrate this shipment of aid from Yerington to Guatemala.

I arrived in Reno, N.V., and was met at the airport by Tom. Since we had never met before, we had much to talk about on the long drive to Yerington. Tom told me the container had arrived and it was huge. The next day, people from Tom's church helped load this huge box. Tom also had inmates from a rehabilitation center help load. Tom drove me to a church member's home in the small town of Yerington. The family was so kind and gave me wonderful hospitality. That night, I went to a high school football game. Tom's

As we entered mom's room, she was sitting on the edge of her bed with legs and feet dangling. Ted picked up a chair and put it directly in front of her.

The first words out of his mouth were, "Clara, have you ever given your life to Jesus?"

I sat at the bottom end of the bed praying, *"Oh no, please God help us to not get thrown out of this room by my mom."*

Mom looked directly at Ted and said, "Well, I think so."

The Lord will accomplish what concerns me.
(Psalm 138:8 NAS)

Ted told Clara a story about a friend of his who received Jesus as his Lord and Savior.

Then he asked, "Clara, do you want to give your life to Jesus today and know definitely that you will live with Him eternally?"

She looked surprised and responded, "Well, yes, I guess so!"

Ted then led her in a prayer for salvation. For some reason, Ted wanted to leave the hospital immediately afterward. I accepted his abrupt request, but when I looked back I saw mom waving at me with one arm and pulling the I.V. stand with the other. It appeared she was trying to follow us. I have wished many times that I would have gone back and given mom a goodbye kiss.

Two days later, we were on a flight to Albania. A Forward Edge International team would join us in Tirana. The team went to conduct a construction and cleanup project for the church in Iba. It was a big job because the building was in much disarray.

I stayed in contact with a member of my family to keep track of mom's condition. Her condition was good one day and not so good another. One day, her condition sounded very poor with a possibility that she wouldn't live through the night. We earnestly prayed about returning home immediately. The next day a report came back that she was doing well, so we decided to stay the last few days with the team in Albania.

On the day we were to leave Albania, our departing flight was canceled. The ticket agent decided to put us on a different airline. Upon check-in, I discovered that the only two seats available on that flight were in first class. Once again we knew God was orchestrating our flights back to the States. Our first stop was in Budapest where we spent the night. The next day we arrived in the U.S. at the Newark airport. I wasted no time telephoning my sister. She told me mom had died the day before. Knowing that God was in charge, total peace came over me.

In everything, by prayer and petition, with thanksgiving, present your requests to God. And the peace of God, which transcends all understanding, will guard your hearts and your minds in Christ Jesus. (Philippians 4:6-7 NIV)

On the day of the funeral, I had the opportunity to share the truth of God's Word with my family. I spoke of how my mom and dad both gave their lives to Jesus just prior to their deaths. I shared how I had confidence I would be united with them for eternity in heaven. The funeral ended and I knew my parents were together forever. I gave praise to Jesus for saving them from all their iniquities and bringing them into His loving arms.

As the months passed, I became more excited knowing my parents were in the presence of the Lord. With a refreshed peace, I took on more responsibilities with new teams arriving in Guatemala.

The Team from Alaska

A team from Alaska came to San Pedro La Laguna with a large donation to bless the brothers for the construction of the elementary school building. Barb and I were at the airport to receive the team of seventeen people who came to help. Some of the women laid block under the supervision of the Guatemala men overseeing the project. The school, when completed, would have four floors of eight classrooms to each floor. It was a big project to undertake and the people from Alaska counted it a privilege to have been involved. At the end of ten days, each team would leave and others would follow.

Barb and I continued to administrate the housing, transportation, and building project for each team. When there were no teams to serve, I would preach among the local churches.

One special Thursday night, I was to preach in a church in Escuintla, Guatemala. As I was praying in my room prior to the meeting, I felt the presence of God. I knew God was going to do something special that night. I cried out for God to receive all the glory.

I spoke out loud, saying, "God, I don't want any person to come to me tonight and say, 'Good job, Don.' Lord, may You receive all the glory, honor, and praise."

Humble yourselves under the mighty hand of God, that He may exalt you at the proper time. (1 Peter 5:6 NAS)

The meeting started at 7 p.m. with an exuberate time of worship. God was surely being exalted. With His name being praised, His glory filled the room. When it was time for me to preach, I brought the word that the Holy Spirit put on my heart. At the end of the message, I gave an invitation for people to come and receive a touch from God. Many came forward. The Holy Spirit was healing and touching many in the room. The musicians began to worship the Lord again. Chairs were folded up and people began dancing and praising the Lord.

It was after ten-thirty when the pastor went up on the platform to close the meeting. The more he tried, the louder it got. He finally gave up and stepped down. People were dancing, singing, and praising God.

I walked to the back of the building, leaned up against a post and said, "Lord, I don't understand. Not one person said good job, Don, or any other compliment."

God responded, "I thought you wanted Me to receive all the glory."

I felt bad and asked God to forgive me. By midnight, many people were on the floor crying, laughing, and praying. Worship continued until one-thirty in the morning. I was stirred watching God's people being moved by His power. My thoughts went to the deep love God has for His people. Wherever Barb and I traveled, we experienced these great movements of God.

India

We returned home and began thinking about an upcoming trip to India. It was suggested by Joseph Anfuso to consider going there to visit various places where he had traveled in the past. It appeared God was opening a door into India. I set the dates for our travel after contacting the brothers in different locations of India and putting together an itinerary.

Several months later, we were on our way to India. We arrived in Mumbai, where we would spend our first three days. After forty minutes of pushing our way to the front of the line, we were finally cleared to enter the country. Several brothers met us at the airport and transported us to a hotel for the night.

It was ten a.m. the next day when two Indian brothers came to visit us and share their ministry. They told us that their Pastor Joseph was the senior leader of hundreds of churches of different denominations in India. They shared that each church was independent in itself and carried its own name, but were all under the leadership of the one senior pastor and his team. I thought, *How great it is when churches of different denominations work together for God's glory.*

How good and how pleasant it is for brethren to dwell together in unity! (Psalm 133:1)

The next morning, we were at one of the churches where God had opened the door for me to preach. The church was amid a community of miles of poverty. About two hundred people attended the service that morning. The Holy Spirit spoke through me and many responded to God's Word.

One young church member testified how God had provided tennis shoes for him that week. It was during the rainy season and many of his family's personal belongings were damaged or washed away. The young man prayed for a new pair of tennis shoes and when he woke up the next morning, there was a pair of tennis shoes still in the box for him. I was touched listening to him. Back in the States, when someone wanted tennis shoes they just go buy them. In India, they go to their Father in heaven asking Him for shoes and He provides. I discovered how real God is to these people.

The next day, we flew to Hyderabad, India. John and Jayamani Kolluri met us at the airport to transport us to their orphanage in Jangon. Brother John, a man God has used to raise up and care for over five hundred churches, was quiet and humble. But when he spoke, much wisdom, power, and revelation came from his lips.

We traveled for four hours over rough, narrow, dangerous roads and highways to arrive at their orphanage in Jangon. More than 250 children resided there. When the orphanage gates opened, the children were lined up in two long rows singing songs of welcome to these two foreigners from a land far away. When we got out of the vehicle, several flowered leis were put around our necks. Then everyone went into a building and sat on the floor. We shared briefly with the children. After a short while, the children were directed to their bedrooms and we were taken to a hostel where we would stay the next three nights.

Arriving at the hostel in the dark, we were led by candlelight to the second floor by Jayamani. It was twenty-five steps to get to the second-floor landing. Each step made creaking noises. On the landing at the top of the stairs, Jayamani opened two huge doors to the bedroom. They made loud screeching noises making the moment very uneasy. There was a big double bed in the middle of the room and an open doorway into another bedroom that had another large double bed in the middle of the room.

We asked, "Why are the beds in the middle of the room?"

Jayamani did not know and bid us, "sleep well." I spotted a door going into a bathroom. With my flashlight in hand, I went in to use the toilet. As I entered the bathroom, some kind of animal ran around the wall of the room and out the window that had no glass in a small part of it. I used some of the water in the bucket that Jayamani had brought up earlier to flush the toilet. Coming out of the bathroom, Barb said she also needed to use the bathroom.

I was pretty certain the animal I saw was a rat, so I said, "Why don't you wait until morning to use the bathroom?"

She insisted she needed to use the bathroom now, so I told her I would stand outside with the door cracked open, sticking my flashlight into the room to give her some light. She agreed and I said nothing to her about the animal I had seen in the bathroom. We crawled into bed with covers over our heads and fell asleep.

Waking up early the next morning, we saw the reason the bed was in the middle of the room. Every creature that God ever created was on the walls of those two rooms. It was a majestic sight! We had a great laugh over what we saw.

There is no fear in love, but perfect love casts out fear.
(1 John 4:18)

At our first breakfast in India, Jayamani explained how the hand and fingers were God's original fork. She then gave us real U.S. utensils. We were delighted she understood the U.S. culture. Shortly after breakfast, we were transported to a large lake area, about a three-hour drive. I was to preach to two hundred people about living a life of faith. I asked brother John how long I should preach and was told no less than an hour and fifteen minutes.

The building they used was small and everyone sat on the floor listening as I preached God's Word. Each time I spoke a scripture, someone would stand up and recite the same scripture from the Bible. When I finished preaching, brother John and several other brothers, baptized many Christians in the lake. It was dark when we returned to the hostel. Our bed looked very accommodating.

John and Jayamani planned our next day's agenda. After breakfast, we traveled to a location where we sat in a shaded area while drinking tea and eating cookies. Then something strange happened. Six men brought a huge, two-wheel cart with two-ten-foot-long beams projecting out from the front of it. The two wheels were more than eight feet in diameter. It was decorated with beautiful flowers from the carriage to the canopy over the top of the seating area. They asked us to climb up into it. Then they brought two large oxen to pull the cart.

All the residents from the town were Christians and they all came out to be part of the festivities. It was an amazing adventure for us, being seated in the cart high above every head, pulled by the oxen. It brought memories of David bringing the ark of God from the house of Obed-edom to the City of David with rejoicing before the Lord. About every ten minutes, the procession would stop and great shouts of praise and exuberant dancing would begin and last for five to ten minutes. The procession continued until we arrived at the location where the meeting was to be held.

David. . . danced before the LORD with all his might, while he and the entire house of Israel brought up the ark of the LORD with shouts and the sound of trumpets. (2 Samuel 6:14-15 NIV)

After the procession reached its destination, more wonderful worship followed. I preached for over an hour and a half. More than seven hundred people attended from villages around the town.

John and Jayamani and the town's people rejoiced over the victory of the Vacation Bible School that just ended. More than 100,000 children attended this two-weeklong function. Several children from each grade level gave testimony of the goodness of God in their lives during that two-week VBS.

After the meeting ended, lunch was served outside to everyone. They all sat on the ground, back to back, in rows of fifty or more. Barb and I each sat on a chair and ate rice from a green leaf plate held flat in the palm of our hand. After lunch, John, Jayamani, Barb, and I traveled to another small town where an American Missionary, Mary Slater, with her husband and children, had raised up a medical clinic and hospital to serve the community.

Mary Slater is held in high esteem for all the medical work she spent her life doing in India. Her work at the clinic and hospital continues, though she has gone home to be with the Lord. There is now a home for the elderly and a thriving village where the people were once beggars. They no longer live in tents but in white houses and have jobs to raise income for their families.

John and Jayamani took us into the house where Mary Slater and her family once lived. John asked me to share a word with the people. After I finished speaking, the people who came into the house knelt to pray. During prayer, I opened my eyes and saw a snake crawling into the center of the group. When I mentioned the word snake it seemed like everyone was scrambling to get outside. Then someone picked the snake up and took it outside to dispose of it. The people then returned to the house and knelt to pray again. When the prayer time ended, John motioned for us to leave.

In the vehicle, John asked me if we were able to visit one more small community that night. When I said yes, we drove for more than an hour and came to a small village with no electricity. It was cold and dark. When the people of the village heard John on the street, they came out of their homes to listen. In deep darkness, John introduced Barb and me to the people and asked me to share God's Word. Though I couldn't see my Bible, I shared God's Word. Then we all went into one of the houses and used an oil lamp to light up the room. I spoke on Jesus asking His disciples, "Where is your faith?" (Luke 8:25).

As we left the village on the way back to the hostel, I fell asleep. On entering the hostel, we passed through the kitchen to our room, we heard two small animals running around the walls. Barb was petrified. It was then I told her about the animal in the bathroom our first night in the hostel.

We slept with covers tightly over our heads, then rose early to pack our luggage. While we had breakfast on the front porch, our luggage was brought down and put in the vehicle. Soon we were on our way back to the airport and said goodbye to our new friends.

Our experiences with John and Jayamani were a gift from God. We learned so much from these two people about dedication to God and His People. John was raised in the same orphanage that he and Jayamani now direct. In addition to the orphanage, John and Jayamani raised up a ministry covering more than five hundred churches, a home for the elderly, an elementary school, a high school, medical help for the poor, and other ministries. God has used John and Jayamani to always press forward in their faith on their way to the victory line.

I press toward the goal for the prize of the upward call of God in Christ Jesus. (Philippians 3:14)

After leaving John and Jayamani, we traveled to Kolkata. Rajib Arohan, a young man who faithfully served Pastor Anjon Sing, met us at the airport and transported us to our hotel in a taxi. Anjon had our itinerary laid out for us and Rajib was to look after our every need.

The day after our arrival, Pastor Anjon asked me to share teachings with many of his pastors and leaders. I was pleased to accept the invitation and spoke about knowing Jesus.

"You know the way to the place where I am going." Thomas said to him, "Lord, we don't know where you are going, so how can we know the way?" Jesus answered, "I am the way..." (John 14:4-6 NIV)

I was to preach in Pastor Anjon's church that evening. Arriving at the Baptist church of about three hundred people, I took off my shoes at the door following the example of everyone else. I had never experienced this before. Immediately after the message, Pastor Anjon and I were the first to go out the front doors to greet each person as they were leaving. After the meeting that night, we took time to be with Rajib and listen to his story. He was a single man, expecting to get married soon. He shared how he lived in a small room with several other men sleeping on the floor without a mattress. He lived on a meager income but gave thanks to God for being able to serve Him.

God put it on my heart to invite Rajib to come to the U.S. and study in a discipleship training program made available through our church. The church would cover his expenses for the nine months he would be in America. When I gave Rajib the invitation, he was overwhelmed. He knew he needed to speak to God, his family, and his fiancée about his decision. His head was spinning with hopes that this would be God's will for his life.

On several occasions during our time in Kolkata, I tried to give Rajib money for extra expenses incurred during our stay. Rajib continuously refused to accept any gift. So, we put money into a sealed envelope and gave it to him just prior to entering the airport building. We allowed no time for Rajib to refuse the envelope. We made sure Rajib was blessed for taking care of us while we were in Kolkata.

By God's grace, Rajib came to the U.S. for those nine months of training. Prior to leaving India, he married his fiancée. After finishing the nine months course, he returned home and has raised up more than fifty churches in India. He and his team of brothers have also raised up his own discipleship training program for church leaders. Many ministries of mercy have been established to serve in his country and elsewhere.

God has used us to bring together many men and women with God's calling on their lives. Rajib, John, and Jayamani received rewards from God too numerous to count. Seeing these blessings on our lives and others, we were excited to see what new venture God had planned for us next.

> *He who comes to God must believe that He is, and that He is a rewarder of those who diligently seek Him.* (Hebrews 11:6)

Chapter 8

TIME OF MIRACLES!

He who is in you is greater than he who is in the world.
(1 John 4:4)

Six weeks after returning from India, we again found ourselves on those pot-holed highways to the interior parts of Guatemala. I was looking forward to arriving in San Pedro Pinula to preach in the Verbo church. The church was small in number, but huge in spiritual matters.

Chepi, my first convert, was asked to give his testimony one Friday evening at the church. He had no education and was void of the Word of God. Prior to conversion, he lived on the streets of San Pedro Pinula and spent his life drinking until the day he gave his heart to Jesus. Now, many months since his conversion, he was to give his testimony of what God did for him. As he began to speak, his voice cracked and he slowly dropped to his knees, crying in thankfulness for what God had done for him. Chepi was a special man of God.

Bicycle Miracle

Barb and I needed to return to Guatemala City by the end of the week to prepare for more travel. As we arrived in the city on our way to the house where we were staying, a child of about nine years old rode his bike directly in front of our vehicle. I was driving about five miles an hour going through a blind intersection when I saw the boy, but it was too late. I heard the clanging of the bike under the scout and the boy disappeared. The next thing I saw was the boy coming out from under the front of our vehicle with his bike. The child jumped on his bike and was gone, never to be seen again. It was a miracle from God that the child wasn't hurt and I wasn't imprisoned.

The incident with the child brought new concerns about driving in Guatemala. We had a team arriving in a few days from the States. Feelings of insecurities began to rise in me as I thought, *"How am I going to be able to drive this team around?"* Then the answer came: I had no alternative. I must drive with extreme caution trusting in the Lord.

Trust in the LORD with all your heart and lean not on your own understanding. (Proverbs 3:5)

Healing Miracles

A team arrived from our church in Union, Missouri. The eleven team members were transported to Casa Bernabe orphanage. Upon arriving there was a short meeting concerning the agenda for the next few days. I shared that it was the practice of F.E.I. teams to rise early each day for a prayer meeting with times of praise and worship. Someone would then share a word with the team for a few minutes.

It was a beautiful morning and the sound of the team's corporate prayer and worship echoed throughout the building. The complete team was circled in a large activity room. Barb and I were scheduled to leave at 10 a.m. traveling over rough roads to arrive by 2 p.m. in a town called Guazacapan. It is a small, coastal town in an extremely hot climate. It only rains there from June to November. The other six months are dry and hot.

Sitting within the circle, a leader's wife began to prophesy over our weekend. She said that we were going to travel to a village where it would be very cold and wet and God was going to heal many people.

I knew the destination we would be traveling to, and since it was in the month of April, it would be very hot and dry. Therefore, I didn't have much confidence that the word she spoke was from the Lord.

It was around 2 o'clock in the afternoon when we arrived at the pastor's home in Guazacapan. It was so hot that I had perspiration rolling off me without doing a thing. Alicia, the pastor's wife, offered some ice-cold lemonade. The humidity condensed and rolled off the cold glass.

The lemonade was so delicious and refreshing, I drank three full glasses.

Pastor Manuel and I talked around the kitchen table about the agenda for the weekend. Manuel spoke with confidence of the healings and movements of the Holy Spirit working through the church. People were being stirred and Manuel, with his wife, were excited about what they were sharing that hot day in their kitchen.

It was 4 o'clock when Manuel said that he was going to the church building to prepare for the evening service. I took time for a cold shower, which in that climate, was so exhilarating. After I finished, Barb desired to do the same. Alicia left to walk to the church, which was only three blocks away. Barb was in the shower when I saw some black clouds rolling in. I called to Barb about what I saw and suggested she might want to shower quickly. Within fifteen minutes, it was almost as dark as night. A loud crack of thunder that sounded like someone shot off a cannon erupted. We hurried, doing a fast-walk to the church.

The very second we stepped into the church, buckets of water fell from heaven. The storm lasted for more than 15 minutes. We walked to the front row of chairs where there was another entry door that was open. The wind and rain were blowing in. It began to get cold in the building. I wished I had brought a sweater. The brothers from the church began to close all the windows and doors. As I sat down, I remembered the word that was prophesied over Barb and me that morning. God was confirming His Word through another miracle.

When the service began, it was still cold in the building, again reminding me of the prophetic word I had received. It came to me to instruct the people that Sunday would be a morning of many healings. God said to tell the people to bring the sick for healing.

I was hesitant to speak these words as the thought entered my mind, *What if no one is healed? I will lose my integrity of preaching the word*. So, I didn't go on the platform to bring the prophetic word of healing. I stood next to Barb feeling condemned, for not trusting God.

I was then called up to the front to bring the Word of God. Walking to the front, I knew what I had to do. I was handed the microphone and asked the people to stand. I began to pray for God's message to be revealed. I looked out upon the hungry congregation and brought the prophetic word that I had been stewing over for what seemed like a lifetime. The people began to clap and yell and I began to speak the Word in faith.

When he has brought out all his own, he goes on ahead of them, and his sheep follow him because they know his voice. (John 10:4 NIV)

Saturday was a day of meeting with the youth in the afternoon and the church leadership in the evening. When Sunday came, the church was full of believers, packed wall to wall, front to back. It appeared they came in faith to receive something special from God.

After a special time of prayer, praise, and worship I went to the front to share God's Word. The Holy Spirit was present throughout the church and I heard God's voice saying, "Go and begin to lay hands on the people and I will heal whoever you touch."

A microphone was handed to me with enough extension cord to reach the back of the building. Immediately, I walked to the back and laid hands on an elderly woman to pray for her healing. The miracles began. People were falling under the mighty power of God's Holy Spirit. Many physical problems were healed, along with sicknesses and diseases. I didn't know all that was happening because of the language barrier, but I saw the evidence of the Holy Spirit's presence. Barb and I continued to walk up and down the only aisle in the church touching and praying for God's people to be healed. It was the Holy Spirit doing the work.

The meeting continued for more than three hours. At one point, God told me to have the little children come and make a circle around Barb and me. We were to lay hands on each child to pray for them. Holding each other's little hands, they made a circle around us. I reached out to touch one of the children and they all went down on the floor. Some were laughing, others crying, and it appeared that all were enjoying God's presence. It was an inspiring sight to behold.

I observed a child of about seven years old sitting on her grandmother's lap. The Holy Spirit said, "Tell the child to go and touch a certain middle-aged lady, sitting at the end of the aisle in a certain row and I will heal her."

I obeyed, but the small child didn't want to respond to what I was asking her to do. So I asked the grandmother to go with her grandchild and touch the specific lady and pray for her. When she did, God touched this lady's situation and she began to weep. The grandmother held her tight and allowed the needy lady to weep on her shoulder. God was healing each one that came to be healed. I didn't preach that day, but Barb and I saw another dimension of God's love.

Being filled with the knowledge of God's love on that early Sunday morning meeting in Guazacapan, we reluctantly left on our

Time of Miracles!

way to San Juan Ostuncalco, high in the mountains. The climate there was the opposite of Guazacapan. San Juan Ostuncalco was cold year-round, but the people were warm to Barb and me. They hovered over us as a mother hen over her chicks. It was one of my favorite churches to visit.

A little after noon, Barb and I arrived in the hustling, busy town of San Juan Ostuncalco. Lucky, the pastor's, wife had prepared a steaming hot, spicy meal for us to enjoy with their whole family around the kitchen table. I loved the atmosphere in the kitchen. It was upbeat and filled with laughter and enjoyment. Cayo, the pastor, and I were close friends. We watched out for each other. Cayo had scheduled me to preach that night. No matter how cold it was, the church members were always there with blankets around their legs and feet.

At the table, Cayo shared with me how the church was meeting at 4 a.m., several days each week. They would begin with prayer in the building and then they walked and prayed in the streets. There were twenty to forty people coming for prayer on those days. After thirty minutes on the streets, taking the city for Jesus, they all met back in the church for fifteen minutes of corporate prayer. We loved it and went out with the church the next morning. Meeting with God's people early in the morning, we found a new fulfillment of corporate prayer. We were excited to start an early morning prayer meeting at our home church in the States.

I pray that the eyes of your heart may be enlightened, so that you will know what is the hope of His calling. (Ephesians 1:18 NAS)

Passport Miracle

We needed to return to the Capitol City to prepare for another F.E.I. team arrival in a couple of days. A team of twenty-one dog groomers from the United States were coming to Guatemala to visit the areas where we worked. They were friends and acquaintances from the pet grooming industry. The team was comprised of mostly Christians and some seeking the truth about Christianity.

The first night became difficult when they found out they would be sleeping in bunk beds at the orphanage. Some thought they would be sleeping at a Marriott on beautiful, ten-inch-thick mattresses. When they found out they would be sleeping on a two-inch foam mattress, some wanted to cry. However, their joy erupted as they stacked two or three mattresses on top of each other. Smiles returned as a result of their ingenuity.

Sally Liddick and Gwen Shelly were close friends of ours and strongly supported our work in Guatemala. It was their idea to bring groomers to Guatemala to introduce them to our work among the poor. As they stepped off the airplane, some team members wanted to cry as they saw the level of poverty. Sally and Gwen were two ladies who had a real heart for those in need.

I told them each day there would be a prayer and worship time at 6:30 a.m. We invited all to join us but told them no one is required to come. The first morning I put out twenty-one chairs in a big circle. Five came on time. Then one by one they filtered in and within fifteen minutes every chair was filled. I chuckled inside and felt blessed and hoped others were also.

Each evening there was a church meeting throughout the interior parts of Guatemala. Again, no one from the team was compelled to come, but as the meeting time drew near, one by one, each team member showed up. I knew that the Holy Spirit was moving in their hearts.

The twenty-one team members were transported in two fifteen-passenger vans. The two vans stayed together, following each other. It was dark and there were a lot of vehicles on the mountain road traveling to San Pedro La Laguna. I felt I had not made a good decision to travel on the highways with two vans full of foreigners at night. I prayed for God's protection all the way.

We all arrived safely in Panajachel at 9:30 p.m. I gave thanks to God for His protection on the highways. I had made reservations at the Grand Hotel for the team to rest that night. The hotel was a great blessing to each team member. It was clean, safe, and had good beds. It was also in the middle of the tourists shopping area. After check-in, the team was on the streets of Panajachel. I suggested they walk two or more together and be careful about what they eat.

In the morning, I took the team to Lake Atitlan, which is at the farthest end of Panajachel. There are twelve towns that surround the lake, each supposedly having the name of one of the Apostles. We boarded a ferryboat to San Pedro La Laguna, a village where I took many teams to serve the needy. It took an hour and a half to cross the lake arriving a little before 11 a.m. Everyone received their hotel room assignment, unpacked, and went in search of a good restaurant. That evening I was to preach in a large church located high up in the mountainous town.

I had asked everyone to give me their passports to keep in a single, safe place. I had my briefcase with the twenty-one passports in it, strapped around my neck while I was waiting for a taxi on the street corner near the hotel. Getting tired of the briefcase over my neck, I took it off and set it down on the street corner. When a taxi came, I got in but forgot the briefcase.

I arrived at the church in time for the service to begin. I preached and many responded to God's call. As the meeting ended, I returned to the hotel and realized my briefcase was nowhere to be found. I began to panic. How could I do such a thing as lose my briefcase with twenty-one foreign passports? Then I remembered there was also $2,000 hidden in a secret compartment inside the briefcase. *What am I going to do?* I thought. *I can't tell anyone what I did or they will think terrible of me. What am I going to do?*

> *"Am I now trying to win the approval of men, or of God? Or am I trying to please men? If I were still trying to please men, I would not be a servant of Christ."* (Galatians 1:10 NIV)

Finally, I gathered everyone together and owned up to my terrible error. They all wanted a piece of my hide, but before they killed me, we all scattered in different directions looking for the briefcase.

About forty-five minutes later, an angel from heaven called out, "I found it."

What a beautiful sound to hear. I couldn't believe it. Praising God, I ran to the hotel lobby. There on the counter, I saw that beautiful briefcase. Looking inside, there were the twenty-one passports and the $2,000 was in the secret compartment. I thought, *God you are so good.*

Apparently, a drunk saw the briefcase, picked it up, went to the hotel lobby, and told them he found this on the sidewalk. The lobbyist received the briefcase and the rest is history. I was grateful to the lobbyist and gave her a reward. I wanted to give the drunk a reward also, but I couldn't find him. The team surrounded me and for some reason, they all wanted their passports back. I handed each team member their passport.

After ten days of traveling in Guatemala, the team boarded the plane back to the States. Barb and I returned home a few days later. We were ready for a time of rest, but we were also looking forward to traveling to Albania later in the fall.

Albania

The colors of the trees and vegetation were beginning to show it was fall when our trip to Albania began. Our ten-hour flight seemed to pass quickly. It wasn't long before the captain was notifying the passengers we would be arriving soon in Tirana. Barb and I were traveling there strictly to be a blessing and an encouragement to the people of Albania.

Pastor Memli and his wife, Luiza, welcomed us at the airport and shuttled us to our sleeping quarters at a ministry center in Tirana. Memli had my agenda for the upcoming days already planned.

The next day, the four of us boarded a public service bus in route to Memli's parents home, three and a half hours away. Pastor Memli's father was in the hospital and needed surgery. I didn't understand what surgery his father needed, but I knew it was a serious time in Memli's father's life.

The following day, Memli invited us to visit his father. We boarded a bus and arrived at the hospital a short time later. A ten-foot-high fence surrounded the hospital with three layers of barbed wire at its peak. There were hundreds of people around the entrance making every effort to pass through the gate to visit some loved one inside. When we arrived, we were told only immediate family members were allowed in to visit his father. We were disappointed but decided to go across the street to purchase a Pepsi. We sat on the curb enjoying our drink as we waited for Memli.

Memli, being taller than anyone else in the crowd around the entry gate, could easily be seen by us. After just a few minutes of sitting on the curb and drinking our Pepsi, we saw Memli's hand motioning for us to come to him.

We disposed of our drinks and hurried to Memli. He told us to stay close to him because the man in front of him was going to help us get through the gate. I grabbed the back of Memli's shirt and Barb grabbed my hand. With such a large crowd pushing and shoving, we could press forward only inches at a time. Finally, we were through. The man that made our entry possible veered off to the right while Memli and Barb continued walking toward the hospital steps. I stood watching the man to see where the man might be going because there were no buildings off to the right.

Memli called out to me, but I kept watching as the man passed in back of a huge tree about fifty feet away from us. I kept watching for the man to come out from behind it, but he never did. It seemed he just vanished. Memli motioned for me to come, but I kept looking at the tree as I walked toward Memli and Barb. No one passed beyond it. God made a way for us when there seemed to be no way.

"I will even make a road in the wilderness and rivers in the desert." (Isaiah 43:19b)

Entering the hospital, we saw it didn't live up to the sanitation standards found in the United States. It appeared there was a shortage of the essentials of life, such as food, sheets, covers, and pillows. These essentials were to be brought in by family members who were allowed to visit. The hospital appeared to be understaffed by medical professionals as well. It also seemed to need administrative and maintenance help. Our eyes were opened to a different set of standards that are taken for granted by those living in the United States.

We saw several members of Memli's family huddled together talking for a long time about what seemed to be a serious issue. Standing in the hallway in front of the doors that led to the operating room, I asked Memli what they were talking about. Memli told me they were trying to raise enough money between them to pay the doctor to perform the operation. When I asked how much the operation would cost, Memli said L (Lek) 6,767.00 which equaled $67.00. I felt so bad for them that they didn't have that small amount of money between them. I asked Memli to allow us to pay for the operation. Memli had difficulty with that offer but when I insisted, Memli took the request to his family and they were so thankful to God.

The operation was successful. Immediately after Memli's father gained consciousness in the recovery room, he asked to see Barb and me. With tears in his eyes, he held my hand tightly and thanked us both. He made us feel like we just gave him our whole life savings. Even the doctor came out and wanted to shake our hands and thank us for helping this needy family.

We remained with Memli's mom in her small, quaint house for two more days after the operation. Memli continued visiting his father in the hospital and taking all the essentials his father needed. He also brought home good reports from the hospital. His father was doing well and growing stronger.

At the end of our stay, I knew God's presence was with the whole family in a new way. After three full days of encouragement and support for Memli and his family, we boarded the bus with Memli and Luiza to return to their home in Tirana.

We continued visiting the growing church in Tirana until the day came to leave for the States. We said goodbye and boarded our flight for home. We knew it was God who had called us to come with blessings and encouragement to honor His people in Albania.

Earthquake in El Salvador

We had been home for only a few days when news of a devastating 7.7 magnitude earthquake struck El Salvador on January 13, 2001. Just a month later, on February 13, a second 6.6 magnitude earthquake struck nearly the same location. These two earthquakes together caused more than 1,200 fatalities with thousands of victims critically injured. Hundreds of businesses and homes were totally destroyed.

Upon hearing of the devastation, we purchased tickets to return to Guatemala to pick up our vehicle and drive to San Salvador, the capital of El Salvador. The drive from Guatemala City took about four hours. I wanted to appraise the damage to know how F.E.I. could help with team support.

After we arrived in San Salvador, I was asked to preach on Sunday morning. I felt honored as I was introduced to the Chief of Police of San Salvador who attended the meeting. For the next three days, the Chief of Police escorted us to the devastated areas. After seeing much of the destruction, I knew that F.E.I. could be a great blessing to this ravaged land.

We planned to drive back to Guatemala City early the next morning but discovered the highway was closed to traffic leaving the country because of mudslides caused by the earthquakes. The highway would be open for traffic leaving the country after 2 p.m. in the afternoon. I asked the Chief of Police about another route to take driving back to Guatemala. I was told to be at a certain intersection at 6 a.m. and he would give us a police escort back to Guatemala.

The sun was beginning to rise when we arrived at the designated intersection. Two police vehicles were already on site. One was a police pickup truck with four policemen in the back and three in the cab. The other police vehicle was a black sedan with two policemen in the front seat and two in the back. One policeman told me to stay a safe distance behind the pickup.

The two police vehicles switched on their flashing, red and blue lights along with their sirens. One was positioned in the front of our vehicle and the other followed behind. For more than fifty miles, we felt like the President of El Salvador. We laughed and shouted how God must have a great sense of humor to allow us to have such an experience.

Arriving in Guatemala, I telephoned Joseph Anfuso to give him a verbal report of the devastation in El Salvador. Immediate plans were discussed for sending team support to serve the victims of the earthquakes. It wasn't long before the first team arrived and two weeks later the second team was on site. They built new homes to replace those that were destroyed and rebuilt small homes that were damaged. When it was time for the teams to leave, much progress had occurred in the devastated areas.

Upon returning to El Salvador at different times, we watched the restoration of lives in progress. We saw towns and villages being rebuilt and made to look new. As we spoke with the people, we saw smiles on faces and joy in the hearts of victims who had faced many hardships.

We enjoyed serving those in need. God had our work cut out for us and soon we would be off to another far-off land to help those with the most serious poverty yet known to us.

Chapter 9

ILLEGAL IN THE CONGO

The LORD spoke to Moses, saying, "Send men to spy out the land of Canaan, which I am giving to the people of Israel." (Numbers 13:1-2)

We flew to England to meet with Richard and Janet Bartrop. The four of us were to travel together and join other leaders in preparation for ministry in three African nations. Richard and Janet had worked with the Zambians for many years. Among other works, they raised up ministries for children in desperate situations. Richard had asked me to come to Zambia and work with him at conferences in several adjoining Zambian nations.

After arriving in Lusaka, the capital city of Zambia, we stayed the night at a ministry center in the heart of the city. It was clean and suitable for the first night there. I looked forward to the days ahead that Richard had planned for us.

The first morning in Lusaka, we met with Richard and Janet and began discussing our plans for the day. After breakfast, we began our journey to the next ministry center in Mwinilunga. The highway we traveled was filled with chug holes. I was reminded of the roads in Guatemala, but these Zambian roads were much worse. It was up and down, in and out, side to side, start and stop. Six hours later, our vehicles turned onto a dusty dirt road that could defy the sandstorms of the Sahara.

After being deluged in dust for fifteen minutes, we arrived at the ministry center. We felt blessed our eyelids were still functioning. Barb and I were given a cabin that looked inviting. However, when I went into the bathroom to use the facility, on the wall directly in front of me, a mere twelve inches from my nose, was a horde of huge spiders. The wall was covered with them. Quickly exiting the bathroom, I went to Richard asking for a different room and received one. While lying in bed, I looked up and saw another spider on the ceiling. Pulling the covers over my head, I went to sleep.

The next morning, Barb stayed with the women and I went with Richard and three Zambians. We left Mwinilunga and traveled for about an hour to the border of the Congo. At the border, Richard and two of the Zambians went into the Congo immigration office. They were there for more than an hour.

"Why is it taking so long?" I asked the young man who stayed with me in the truck, but he didn't know.

It was midday when our passports were returned to us and we were told we were free to go. We traveled through the jungle to the interior parts of the Congo. By 6:00 p.m., we arrived in a small village where we met a Congo pastor who offered us hospitality for the night. Richard went into one bedroom and I went to another.

My bed was about four inches too short, so I laid diagonally on the bed so most of my feet were under cover.

An exterior door going outside of my bedroom was left open. Just as I was dozing off to sleep, I heard what sounded like an animal coming into the bedroom through the open door. It was very dark, so I could not see, but just before the animal nibbled on my exposed toes, I heard the bellow of a goat. Tucking my feet under my butt and pulling the covers over my tucked in body, I slept like that the rest of the night.

He who dwells in the shelter of the Most High will rest in the shadow of the Almighty. (Psalm 91:1 NIV)

The next morning, I was awakened early by cows mooing, dogs barking, and goats bellowing. The pastor kindly prepared breakfast for everyone before we headed out for more jungle travel. The day was a long one. The road was no more than a dirt path, yet there were eighteen police checkpoints. Most of the soldiers at the checkpoints had no uniforms. They barely had clothes. At each checkpoint, they would go through three or four suitcases looking for weapons and asking for food.

At the first fourteen checkpoints, no one opened my suitcase. I was happy about that. Then I became uneasy when one of the soldiers picked up my suitcase and opened it. I thought, *Oh no, these guys are going to see all my snacks.* When they saw all the cupcakes, brownies, candy, and beef jerky, they all started laughing.

"He's got enough for an army," somebody said as they started helping themselves.

Smiling, I said, "I brought this for you guys. So just enjoy! Hey, could I have a brownie, though?"

Around 3:00 p.m., we arrived in a small town called La Muchacha. The driver was told to stay at the truck with me. The two Zambians and Richard went into the immigration office to get approval for the conference. After nearly an hour waiting in the blazing heat, the three came out of the office and we headed out through the jungle on another dirt path.

The driver and I were laughing and telling funny stories. Not paying attention to what he was doing, the young driver ran the pickup off the path into a mud swamp. Nothing our group of five did was able to move the pickup. It was by God's grace that we were only a fifteen-minute walk from where the conference was to take place. Four of us stayed with the truck while the driver went ahead to the conference site to get help. He returned with more than forty helpers. Everything was unloaded out of the back of the truck, then they made a circle around the truck, lifted it, and carried it back on the path. Everyone cheered!

We jumped back in the vehicle and headed for the conference site, sticking our hands out the truck windows, touching those who were walking and running alongside us. More than five hundred natives met us at the conference site. So many were pushing against us to touch our white skin, it left a big dent in the side of the truck. The welcoming party finally dispersed and we were able to unload the truck and eat dinner.

The conference site was a big, grass field. There were no chairs to sit on or lights to light up the area. A generator was brought in the back of the pickup to operate the sound system and to light up the pulpit with one forty-watt light bulb. Praise and worship began with a degree of exhilaration I had not encountered before. The attendees were dancing, singing, and praising the Lord with all their might. Dust was flying and hands and arms were waving high unto the Lord. It was so dark I could barely see the first six rows of people.

I started preaching about 9:30 p.m. and then gave an invitation for people to come forward to receive healing as I closed my teaching. It looked like all 1,000 people were trying to come to the front at the same time. They were hungry for the Lord and looking for a miracle. Many were pushing and shoving. The meeting nearly turned into mob chaos. Ushers were quickly selected to allow only ten people at a time to get through to the front. By the time we finished ministering, it was well after midnight.

The next morning began at 7:00 a.m. with breakfast outside under God's beautiful blue sky. There were many large trees in the area that provided a cool breeze and shade. I spent time before the Lord preparing for the first two sessions. Richard would take the next two sessions, then I would follow with two more sessions until midnight rolled around again. Richard asked me to repeat the message I had shared the night before, but this time with props familiar to the people such as pots, pans, lids, forks, spoons, and knives to bring more clarity to the word.

Each session began with that joyful time of praise and worship. More than a thousand people attended each session. Some walked for more than a week to be at this conference. As I concluded my midafternoon session, the Holy Spirit instructed me to take the people in a procession formation and march around the area. I told them to do whatever they saw me do. If I raise my hands, everyone else should raise their hands. If I jumped to the left and then to the right, everyone else did the same. It was a great time of fun with the Lord. We all enjoyed this Spirit-led activity.

Those three days passed quickly. They were events I would never forget. An offering was taken for Richard and me, which we accepted and then gave it to the ministry of the Congo. Then we packed all our belongings and traveled that whole day through the jungle arriving at our next location around 4 p.m. where three more days of the conference were to take place.

It was a practice in the African Congo to cover the road with flowers when a high-ranking government official was entering a town. When the Toyota entered the village at the conference site, flowers covered the road. Though we were not high-ranking government officials, we were a royal priesthood representing the holy nation of the Kingdom of God. The roads were covered with every colored flower available. The people sang, danced, and praised the Lord in front of our vehicle as we drove into the town and up to the conference site. Though we knew we did not deserve this kind of honor, the Lord was blessing us for coming.

You are a chosen people, a royal priesthood, a holy nation, a people belonging to God, that you may declare the praises of him who called you out of darkness into his wonderful light.
(1 Peter 2:9 NIV)

I was again asked to take the first night's session and had another wonderful time with the Congolese people. I was also asked to take the third and fourth session the next day. We preached under a temporary pavilion that had a thin layer of straw spread over the roof to shade the people from the heat of the midday sun.

When the meeting ended late that night, three young men in their twenties came to me requesting to talk to me about something important. I told them I could meet with them in the morning as I was free during the first two sessions. However, the next morning Richard asked me to take the first two sessions. I forgot about the three young men who wanted to speak with me.

At the end of the second session, I jumped into the truck with the team to go to the house for lunch. Five young men came to me and reminded me of my commitment to talk with them. They looked desperate.

I thought it was about money, but when I got out of the truck and asked them what they wanted they replied, "Who is this Holy Spirit you spoke about last night and how do we get Him?"

I told the team members to go on without me and took the five inquisitive men back under the pavilion. The five sat on the ground and I sat on a short stool as I taught them about the Holy

Spirit. The Holy Spirit gave me one thought after another and one scripture after another.

After about thirty minutes they asked, "Can we receive Him now?"

I began to pray for them to receive the Holy Spirit. As I went to lay my hand on one of them, they all fell on the ground at the same time, some crying, some laughing, some praying. Seeing the sincerity of these five young men's love for God and their deep desire for more of the Holy Spirit, made my journey to the Congo more valuable than life itself.

For two and a half more days, the conference continued. Great times of ministry exploded during moments of praise, worship, and the preaching of God's Word. The people came hungry for the Word and God fed each one accordingly.

When it was time to return to Zambia, we traveled for about five hours and came to the Congo-Zambia border. There was no difficulty entering Zambia. We were on the Zambian highway driving towards Mwinilunga when we heard a news report on the radio about two white foreigners who had not been taken into custody yet for entering the Congo illegally. The police were still looking for them.

Richard started laughing and said, "That's us."

Now I understand why it took so long at the Congo border when we first arrived and at the La Muchacha government office to receive permission for the conference there. I also found out that the Congo Visa emblem in my passport was an outdated one. Apparently, our whole eleven days in the Congo were administratively illegal.

God's protection was over us.

The last day of our time in Mwinilunga was spent teaching in a one-day conference. At the end of the last session, my wife and I returned to the same cabin we were assigned the first day we arrived. While I was in the Congo, Barb and a friend helped to fumigate the cabin from insects with smoke bombs that worked quite well. We rested quietly through the night and were ready to leave in the morning for Lusaka.

About halfway to Lusaka, we left the group to meet up with Ramson and Mercy Mumba, friends we had met in England two years prior. It was a wonderful time of reconnecting and listening to them tell about their life in Zambia. We then traveled to Lusaka the next day on a bus. After a bit of touring, the rest of the group flew to Zimbabwe, but Barb and I decided to rest in Lusaka for two days then fly to Zimbabwe on Sunday. In Lusaka, I was able to spend time with Roma Nyakambumba who had an apostolic ministry overseeing churches in Zambia and the Congo.

Roma asked me, "How much money did you commit to during your stay with us here in Zambia and the Congo?"

"Nothing!" I responded.

"Wonderful!" said Roma. "That's not the norm, but it's great."

He told me how some groups come promising financial support, hoping to build a ministry among the churches. Sometimes this brings confusion or even hurt. Roma and I had an informative time together.

Early Sunday morning, Barb and I bought our tickets and flew to Zimbabwe to meet up with the rest of the team. Our flight landed at 9:25 a.m. A brother from Covenant Ministries was there to take us directly to the church. We arrived just a few minutes before the service began and were led to the front row of chairs. The pastor looked straight at me and asked me to come and bring God's Word. I knew God opened this door for me to bring a message and give an invitation for the people to come and receive a touch from God. Barb and I prayed for many that morning.

The next day, we left Zimbabwe to fly back to the States. After a busy year, we felt that it was time to go home to rest and wait upon the Lord to receive direction for future opportunities to minister. It was evident that God was preparing us to send larger quantities of aid to underdeveloped nations.

Members of our family came to the airport to welcome us home. The summer months were still hot in St. Louis, but the beautiful colors of fall were quickly closing in. Arriving at our home in Wildwood generated good memories of family activities.

We received an invitation to attend a special meeting being held at a church in North St. Louis. When we arrived, we discovered the meeting was a fund-raising event to support the additional construction of a new building for the church. The pastor brought a message on giving. Barb and I began praying about what God wanted us to do. I wanted to commit $5,000 to the project but heard nothing from God. When I leaned over and asked Barb if God had put anything on her heart, she said she had heard nothing.

The pastor began calling row-by-row forward for each one to commit to the amount they felt God was putting on their hearts. When our row was called, Barb and I stayed in our seats. Afterward, I asked God why He didn't have us commit any money for the project. Again I heard nothing. I told Barb I felt terrible and felt everyone was watching me. Barb said she felt the same, but she also told me she knew we did the right thing. We felt the peace of God as we looked to Him and not to man. We didn't understand it, but we knew God was with us.

The LORD does not look at the things people look at. People look at the outward appearance, but the LORD looks at the heart. (1 Samuel 16:7 NIV)

Two weeks passed and we returned to Guatemala. We stayed the first night in the capital city at the home of the brother who brought us our vehicle and then drove to the church in San Juan Ostuncalco the next morning. Shortly after we arrived, Pastor Cayo Cotom took us to see the parcel of land that the church recently purchased. They intended to construct their own church building on the plot. Cayo asked Barb and me to pray with him and those who followed him to the land. The small group dedicated the land to the work of the Lord.

The next morning as we were praying, God put it on my heart that this is where He wanted us to make our offering. When I shared it with Barb, she was in agreement. Getting up from the bed,

I immediately wrote the check for the same $5,000 I had wanted to give to the church in North St. Louis. We were so happy.

God loves a cheerful giver. (2 Corinthians 9:7)

We couldn't wait to give the offering to Pastor Cayo. In less than a month, Cayo's church broke ground to begin construction of the building. Pastor Cayo knew I was thinking about what would happen when the $5,000 ran out, so he shared their plan with me.

Their town had a market day every Sunday from 7:00 a.m. to midafternoon. They decided to have their first service each Sunday morning in the marketplace and then sell hot plates of food and drinks plus things that people had donated. They continued this practice until enough money was raised to finish the construction of the new building. It worked! God blessed their endeavor. With donations that came in from various sources and from their hard work of selling food and donated items, they never ran out of money for the construction project and finished in a little more than a year.

God was in control.

We continued traveling among the churches in the capital city and returned home at the end of the year to be with our family during the Christmas holidays. In late winter, we saw that the aid was multiplying by leaps and bounds. The warehouses in Downingtown, Pennsylvania; Wentzville, Missouri; and Yerington, Nevada were beginning to overflow with relief aid. I put together an agenda to send the aid to Guatemala from these three locations as soon as possible. We acquired a warehouse in Guatemala City to use for three days to store the aid and divide it among twenty-seven different churches throughout Guatemala City and the interior parts of the country. The warehouses held hospital beds, examining tables, wheelchairs, crutches, clothing, shoes, toys, bicycles, a new cement mixer, furniture, and many household items.

Along with this aid, I had great favor with the new government of Guatemala. The wife of the president of Guatemala sent Barb and me an invitation to come to the palace that she might meet us. She wanted to help us to be able to bring this aid into Guatemala without paying taxes on the relief goods.

We flew to Pennsylvania to help load two containers and ship them out of the east coast. We returned to St. Louis to load another container in Wentzville, Missouri, and ship it out of New Orleans. Lastly, we flew to Yerington to load and ship the fourth container out of Los Angeles, California, to the west coast of Guatemala. We then returned to Guatemala to receive all four containers, unload them, and help in the distribution of the relief aid.

A team of fourteen young adults from Sacramento, California, came to Guatemala to minister with drama, preaching, and the distribution of the aid. They were transported to Jutiapa, where they began drama skits on the streets while hundreds gathered to watch. At the end of the skits, the Word was preached, and an invitation was given for the unsaved to receive Jesus into their lives. The team enjoyed helping with the distribution of aid. Children, adults, and the elderly received clothing and personal items. Furniture, bicycles, and household items were also given to those in need. God blessed those who gave as well as those who received.

On Sunday morning, the team preached God's Word on a Guatemalan army base to about three hundred soldiers. Many gave their lives to Jesus. The meeting ended with soldiers crowding around the Americans asking questions about God's saving grace. Afterward, the team departed and returned to the homes of those who had given us hospitality. Some team members prepared more skits for the evening service. Others prepared for their morning return to the Capitol City and to the airport for their return to their homes in the States.

Another new day began as we returned home with the team. Future teams and the collection and sending of aid kept me busy. Barb began to supervise the sorting of the relief aid and its classification according to gender, size, and usage. God had given us this new mission of serving the poor and only He could lead us on the path that lay ahead.

Chapter 10

LIGHT IN DARK PLACES

He will command his angels concerning you to guard you in all your ways. (Psalm 91:11 NIV)

Albania

A war had been brewing in Kosovo from early 1998 to mid-1999. Kosovo was declaring its independence from Serbia. For more than a year after the war ended, many homeless people from Kosovo fled to Albania looking for food, shelter, and protection. Barb and I volunteered to return to Albania to help serve these refugees. Unfortunately, all borders were closed into Albania. Passage was denied at the international airport along with bus and other forms of foreign transportation. It appeared that it might be impossible for us to get into Albania. However, I knew God had spoken to us to go and serve the Kosovo refugees.

Missionary friends of ours working in Albania during this time advised us to fly into Thessalonica, Greece, and make our way to the international bus depot. From there we could buy a bus ticket to the

Greece and Albania border and possibly cross into Albania at that point. The plan sounded good to me, so I began to search for ways to travel from St. Louis, Missouri to Thessalonica, Greece.

Soon after we made our travel plans known throughout the ministry, we received a request from a brother, Leslie Wright, from a church in Chester, England. He desired to travel with us to Albania. Though we did not personally know him, Barb and I were pleased, thinking Leslie was sent by God to help make travel decisions. We were to meet Leslie in England on the Sunday afternoon before our flight to Greece. The three of us would then travel together until our return to England.

The night before we were to leave for Albania, I received a call from the pastor of our church. He asked if I was certain I had heard from God to travel to Albania to serve the refugees of Kosovo. We were confident that God had spoken to us. I knew there was a possibility that we might never return, but we put all those possibilities in the hands of God. We were confident that God was sending us to Albania for His purpose. We purchased our tickets to England and on to Thessalonica, Greece.

> *I have surely seen the oppression of My people who are in Egypt; I have heard their groaning and have come down to deliver them. And now come, I will send you to Egypt.* (Acts 7:34)

Barb and I arrived in England on Friday and met with Leslie on Saturday. A gathering of about twenty-five brothers and sisters came together at a church with the three of us that afternoon. A large circle of chairs was formed and many began sharing God's Word. They began to pray and call upon the Holy Spirit to protect the three of us throughout our travel and work. Many prophetic words were spoken, but one prophecy totally stuck with the three of us: "When someone says go you stop, and when someone says come you go."

Late Sunday evening, we boarded our flight and landed around 11:00 p.m. in Thessalonica. After gathering our bags, we noticed the airport was beginning to close. Within twenty minutes the lights were just about all turned off, so we headed for an exit door. Leaving the building, we stood under an open-air porch with a small forty-watt light bulb trying to give light to an immense dark area. It was now going on midnight. We looked at each other wondering what to do.

Then Barb remembered that before we left the States the brothers told us to make our way to the bus depot after landing in Thessalonica and take a bus to the border of Albania. In a strange country, not knowing a single Grecian word, the three of us needed God's help. Two men came walking around the side of the building where we were standing.

They asked in perfect English, "Do you need any help?"

I said, "We're wanting to go to Tirana, Albania."

The men responded, "Oh, that's where we're going. Come with us."

We looked at each other bewildered.

I asked, "Should we go or not?"

Barb remembered the prophetic word we received in England, "Go if you hear someone say, come."

The decision was then easy based upon God's prophetic word. The two men flagged down two taxicabs. Barb, Leslie, and I rode in one and the two men rode in the other. Twenty minutes later, we entered the parking lot of a bus depot.

I immediately jumped out of our taxi, speaking in a loud voice. "We have no Grecian money!" "Don't worry," said one of the men, "we have enough to pay for both taxicabs."

Upon entering the bus depot, we were told there was just one bus leaving in a few minutes, but only five seats were left and they were all first-class seating. Again, I relayed that I had no Grecian money. Again, one of our new friends said he had enough for all five of us.

Boarding the bus, we found the five first-class seats were in the front of the bus. Since it would be a long journey to the border, the first-class seats were a big blessing from God. After inquiring about the exchange rate from U. S. dollars to Grecian money, I gave the two men the money for the taxi and bus fares.

The three-hour journey ended in a very dark, quiet, deserted area that appeared to be the end of the highway. Everyone disembarked except the three of us. One of the two men told us to stay on the bus until they returned to lead us into Albania. Barb, Leslie, and I sat on the bus in the dark, in the middle of nowhere, with not one person around, not even the driver. We sat there for about twenty minutes, which seemed like hours. Finally, the two men returned to the bus and motioned for us to be quiet and to follow them.

Disembarking in pitch-black darkness, the three of us followed the two men in total quietness through what seemed to be a densely wooded area. Soon, we arrived at a small house and stood outside as a window opened. We were asked by one of our two new friends to give them our passports. We did as we were asked and our two friends proceeded to hand them over to someone inside the house. It was about ten minutes later, which again seemed like hours, the window reopened and the passports were handed back to all five of us.

The five of us began to walk quietly through the wooded area again until we reached a street with buildings. We came upon a van and were asked to get in. It already had about ten people in it. I thought most of them were refugees from Kosovo. We then began a long trip to our final destination in Albania.

After about three hours of traveling through the winding mountain roads of Albania, the van came to a halt in a small town. There our two new friends from Thessalonica disembarked. The three of us were told to stay glued to our seats until the van arrived in Tirana. Doing as we were told, we arrived at our final destination late in the day.

In Tirana, the three of us made our way to the Stephens Center pulling our luggage behind us. This small hotel gave lodging to many missionaries coming to Albania to serve the needy. It was clean lodging and served delicious food from the first-floor restaurant that drew many tired Kingdom workers to its quarters.

We were assigned our rooms and rested well through the night. The next morning, we rose early, ready to serve the Kosovo refugees in different camps. After a tasty breakfast, we walked several blocks and entered a big arena where we saw hundreds of people sleeping on mattresses spread out on the floor and bleachers surrounding the gymnasium. We were assigned to work in the makeshift kitchen and were given instructions on how to slice the bread and distribute the soup. With other volunteers, we began to hand out food and water to those standing in long lines, many with tears waiting patiently to receive nourishment.

We began to help people who had lost everything. Some even lost their husbands, fathers, sons, and friends. Some of the women and young girls were abused by the enemy. For most of them, the only clothes they had were the clothes they were wearing. All had serious needs. Each day, we did this while praying for the needs of the refugees. We also spent time with our friends, Memli and Luiza.

God showed Himself faithful in every adventure in which we found ourselves.

We found our two weeks in Albania flew by fast. During our last day there, Memli suggested he would meet us early the next morning and help us find transportation to a border town of Greece, many hours away. I felt that this would be a great blessing. The following morning at about 3 a.m. the three of us left our rooms at the Stephen Center and looked for Memli, but Memli was nowhere to be found.

I trusted God that nothing went wrong with Memli's plan. I knew how wonderful and faithful a man Memli was. It was not Memli's character to not show up. I knew that something must have happened to prevent Memli from being with us. I hoped and prayed that Memli was all right. Later in an e-mail, Memli told us about a problem with the alarm clock. He had no way of waking up so early, especially after reading and studying God's Word into the wee hours of the morning. I knew that Memli had probably just gone to sleep about the same time that we were waking up.

After waiting for Memli for a short time, the three of us separated and headed up and down different streets looking for a vehicle that had a driver who could take us to Korce, a south-eastern Albanian town near the Grecian border.

At 3:30 a.m., the streets were quiet and empty. Darkness covered the early morning hours. About thirty minutes had passed when I spotted a van a block away. With hands clutched as a megaphone around my mouth, I called out in a loud voice for Barb and Leslie. My voice echoed through the streets until Barb and Leslie came running.

When we looked into the van, Leslie saw a man sleeping in the front seat and Barb saw someone sleeping in the last seat of the van. The three of us then began knocking on the windows. The man in the front seat jumped up, opened his door, and came running out.

I tried to communicate with him that the three of us needed to travel to Korce, and then on to Thessalonica, Greece. No communication seemed to be working until the driver opened the rear passenger door of the van and motioned for the three of us to come and climb in.

We looked at each other, laughing, and Leslie said, "It looks like he's saying 'Come.' That's our sign to go. Let's get in."

We were off and running. We had no idea if the driver knew where we needed to go to get into Greece, but we trusted God was leading us safely there.

By faith Abraham obeyed when he was called to go out. . ., not knowing where he was going. (Hebrews 11:8)

After traveling for a couple of hours, we stopped at a refugee camp in a small town in Albania. We all stepped out of the van to stretch our legs. The young girl and driver went walking through the camp. It appeared like they were looking for a specific person.

Fifteen minutes later, we all stepped back in the van and continued on the winding, two-lane mountainous highways. By this time, Barb had figured out what was happening. We were on a refugee hunt for a relative of the young girl who was now riding in the front passenger seat. After visiting three more camps, the van arrived in Korce in midafternoon stopping directly in front of a bus depot. When we asked the driver the cost of our travel, it took nearly every dollar and English pound we had to pay him. Our wallets were left empty.

As we entered the bus depot, I saw an advertisement in the window promoting Master Card. I was thrilled to purchase our bus tickets on my credit card. The bus to Thessalonica was ready to leave, so we found our seats and relaxed during the last leg of our journey.

Our bus arrived in Thessalonica that evening. We hired a taxi to take us to a hotel near the airport. The next day, we did some site seeing. The following morning, we arrived early at the airport finding our flights to England were on time.

Our two weeks in Albania had passed by quickly and our work had come to an end. We had been a great trio traveling and working together. As we returned to England, Barb and I said goodbye to our good friend, Leslie. We booked a hotel room at the airport, enjoyed an English dinner, and rested for the night.

Guatemala and Argentina

It was late summer when we returned to our home in the States. The heat of the season was dissipating. There was a cool breeze in the air as thoughts of the upcoming ministry to Guatemala and Argentina filled my mind. October rolled around quickly and I was eager to return to colorful Guatemala and prepare the work of receiving three containers of aid for the needy. I also wanted to share my time with some of the churches I had relationships with.

I arrived in Guatemala without Barb. She was to meet me there after my upcoming trip to Argentina. I collected my bags, went through customs, and exited the building. I set my briefcase down on the pavement behind me, and started loading my luggage in the car. I didn't notice my briefcase was missing until I arrived at a church, only a few minutes from the airport. The briefcase held my cameras, cell phone, and laptop. Most of all, I had $5,000 cash in it that I was to deliver to an orphanage. Someone had picked up that briefcase while I was loading the luggage and I never knew it. After many weeks of travel in Central and South America, I looked forward to return home to recoup this money.

In Guatemala, I was blessed to acquire a large warehouse on the outskirts of Guatemala City. It was a great location to unload the containers that were soon to arrive and distribute the aid. Preparations were falling into place. By the middle of the week, all preparations for three containers were completed and I needed to travel to Argentina to share in a leadership conference near Cordoba.

When I arrived there, I was escorted to the pastor's home where I had a delicious meal and enjoyed fellowship with other men of God. I always enjoyed coming to Jose Miguel's house because his wife, Adriana, served the best meal with the tastiest meat in the whole world.

At the end of the week, we traveled to the conference where I shared experiences with pastors and leaders. I took advantage of the opportunity to minister to these men and their wives. In praying with them, I sensed that they were hungry for more of God.

On Sunday evening after the conference, I was invited to share with a large church of about 2,000 members. When I arrived at the building, I was asked to wait in the pastor's office before entering the auditorium. The building accommodated more than 2,100 seats that were tiered down from the back to the front. The platform was seven feet high and seemed to be dangerously high off the floor.

When the worship began, it was glorious. The office was on the opposite side of the thin wall separating it from the auditorium. As I closed my eyes and meditated on the time of worship, the Holy Spirit filled my heart with the love of God. After about forty-five minutes of worship, the elders came and directed me to the auditorium. I was given a seat down on the floor at the right side of the platform. I felt so full of God in the worship hall filled with the people of God. By the time they called me up to bring God's Word to His people, I was so full of God that everything I spoke was coming directly from God's throne-room. Near the end of the message, I gave an invitation for people to come forward and receive Christ, healing or any other need they might have. Hundreds of people came forward to receive more of God.

Because of the late hour, the elders kept trying to get me out of the auditorium, but I kept praying for people. It was well past midnight when I finally finished ministering to God's people. The elders then took me swiftly out of the building along with the pastor. We returned to the pastor's home where I rested that night before returning to Guatemala the next day. There I would receive the containers of aid and distribute them among the poor and needy through the administration of the churches.

The next morning at breakfast, I asked Jose Miguel the cost for a foreigner to leave the country. Jose Miguel said there was an eighteen-dollar tax levied on all people leaving Argentina. I emptied my pockets of all the money I was carrying except for the eighteen-dollar exit fee. I then gave the balance to Jose Miguel for all the kindness shown to me in feeding, driving, and caring for me while in Cordoba.

He may exalt you in due time, casting all your care upon Him for He cares for you. (1 Peter 5:6, 7)

When I arrived at the airport, I went directly to the Continental Airline check-in counter inquiring about my flight to Guatemala. I learned my flight had been canceled. Since I was responsible for the containers that were to arrive at the Port in Guatemala, I felt it was imperative to try to find a way to return to Guatemala even if it were in the middle of the night. I asked the flight attendant at the counter if there was any way to fly a different airline on my ticket. She worked diligently to make it happen and got me on an airline connecting through Chile and arriving in Guatemala the next morning. I inquired about taxes to arrive or leave Chile and was told by the attendant that there were no taxes to pay. That was great news.

When I arrived in Chile, I tried to pass through immigration, but was told there was a one-hundred-dollar tax levied on all U.S. citizens entering or leaving Chile. I had zero money and there was no ATM machine available. I did what any other person would do, I began asking people coming into the country to loan me one hundred U.S. dollars.

"No, no, no!" was all I heard.

It was like asking fish in an ocean not to swim. A policeman walked up to me and asked me what I was doing. I explained it all to him and he then asked to see my passport. I gave the passport to him, but the policemen refused to give it back. As he walked away from me with my passport, I began to pray. About that time, an older American couple walked passed me. I began to tell them my story.

I thought I had found someone who could help me, but after listening to me, the man's wife said, "Come on, George, let's go."

I pleaded with him and even offered to give him my wedding band as collateral. I told him he could send it to me when I sent him the one hundred dollars once I returned home in two weeks.

The American wasn't interested in my wedding ring, but finally said, "Okay, I'll give you the one hundred dollars, but upon getting through, you must get the money from an ATM machine on the other side of immigration."

I thanked him many times and agreed to his terms. Then I located the policeman that was holding my passport and showed him the one hundred dollars the traveler loaned me. The policeman returned my passport with a lecture on why traveling with no money is a bad idea.

With passport in hand, I hurried to the designated window to pay my taxes and pass through immigration. A flight attendant sought me out to help me find my luggage and leave the airport. I looked back and recognized the elderly couple still waiting for their luggage.

Upon leaving the airport, I spotted an ATM machine. I withdrew one hundred and fifty dollars to give to the couple as they came out of the airport. I stood there and waited for them. When they finally came through the doors leading outside, their eyes lit up when they saw me standing there waiting for them. I told them I went to the ATM machine and got one hundred and fifty dollars in the country's denomination and gave them the whole amount. They didn't want the extra fifty dollars, but I insisted. It was my way of saying thank you. I was blessed and so were they.

I acquired a hotel room that night and early the next morning returned to the airport to catch my flight to Guatemala. I was finally on my way to be with the one I loved so much. When I saw Barb waiting for me in the middle of the crowd in Guatemala, my eyes lit up. We had so much to tell each other.

It didn't take long for us to receive word that the containers of aid had arrived and were ready to be unloaded. We spent the weekend distributing the aid to the churches we worked with. After preaching on Sunday, we returned to the States together on Monday.

Several months later, we were asked to return to Argentina to participate in another pastor and leader's conference. Since it was a great experience in the past to be with the brothers in Argentina, we looked forward to those relationships there to grow. We set our agenda to be at the conference in early spring of the upcoming year.

At home, our work was piling up. Barb and volunteers from the church worked three to four days each week at the warehouse in Wentzville. They separated the aid and tested the value of the appliances and furniture to see if it was worth sending. They also inspected clothing and shoes for quality, size, and gender plus other miscellaneous items for their value.

On the day the containers arrived for loading, they were sent to their designated warehouse. I tried to have no less than ten volunteers to help load each container. The warehouses always had an excessive amount of aid causing those who were loading the containers to spend extra time tightly packing them piece-by-piece.

I spent time each day preparing the logistics for shipping the containers. The cost, origin, destination, and bookings caused the paperwork on my desk to look like the wind of a tropical storm hit my office. The work seemed endless as I tried to send the aid to various nations without paying large amounts of taxes and shipping costs upon arrival.

Whatever you do in word or deed, do all in the name of the Lord Jesus, giving thanks to God the Father through Him. (Colossians 3:17)

Transporting goods to the needy always appeared to be a kind gesture and in most cases, it was appreciated. However, there were always those who showed appreciation to us as long as they were getting what they wanted. Their character at times was a bit difficult to work with, but by the end of each day everything seemed to fall into place and no one ever had their feelings hurt.

Argentina

After all the relief aid was distributed through the churches to the needy, we returned to the States and set our itinerary of travel for the next few months. Argentina was at the top of the list because of the earlier invitation and flights already purchased.

A month and a half later, we were on our way to Argentina again. It was early spring in St. Louis and the weather was still a bit chilly, but in Argentina, the weather was expected to be beautiful.

Arriving in Cordoba after a short layover in Bueñas Aires, we were received by Pastor Jose Miguel Aguero. He transported us to a comfortable hotel in the middle of the city and gave us our itinerary for the upcoming days.

I taught in several sessions at the conference with about 125 leaders. The sessions started on a Friday night and went through to 2 p.m. on Sunday afternoon. We rested in a room at the conference center until 7 p.m. when we were transported to a church of about 200 people. The church service took place under a metal roof that had no wall on the left side nor a wall at the back of the building.

The young translator had a difficult time understanding my English as I began preaching a message on "Being Secure In Christ." So, I began to preach in Spanish. I got a little help from the young translator and from a few people in the congregation. It was not an evangelistic message at all. Plus, the confusion of languages only made it worse. I considered it a total loss.

At the end of the message, the Holy Spirit told me to give an invitation for people to receive Christ. I had my doubts about whether I had truly heard from God, but I did as I believed God was telling me. About twelve hands went up. I was startled. I thought they didn't understand my question, so I told them to put their hands down. I tried again to ask the same question, trying to be clearer this time with my Spanish.

"If you have never invited Jesus to come into your life and you want to do that tonight, raise your hand."

More than twenty hands went up. So, I invited all who had their hand up to come forward and receive Jesus into their life. All twenty people came forward plus many more. There were so many people up front that many of them were standing outside beyond the protection of the roof. I called for the church leadership to come up and pray for these people to receive Christ Jesus after I prayed a corporate prayer of repentance and salvation, having the people repeat after me.

There was so much joy under and outside that roof that night. I knew the Holy Spirit fell on those who came forward. I also knew that the meeting wasn't dependent on my Spanish. It was totally dependent on God's people putting their trust in God.

We returned to our hotel for a night's rest before we flew back to the States in the morning. Jose Miguel drove us to the Cordoba airport. Arriving at the ticket counter, we were told we had been put on a later flight to Bueñas Aires. However, that wouldn't work because we would miss our connecting flight to Panama and then another connecting flight to Honduras. The counter attendant told us the next flight out was full. She suggested we wait and see if someone canceled.

We stood for a long time watching another group of people board a flight. I finally inquired of its destination and discovered it would be going to Bueñas Aires. I asked if we could get on that flight. After a few minutes of working on the computer, the attendant told us they had two seats open. We were thankful to God for making a way to Bueñas Aires where there seemed to be no way.

Arriving in Bueñas Aires, a limousine met us on the runway to take us to the terminal. Entering the terminal among hundreds of people, there was a short man holding a sign as high as he could with our names on it.

When we told the man that was our name, he said, "Let's go. We must get you to the international terminal."

The problem was he needed to drive as fast as he could through the city during rush-hour traffic to get us to our flight on time. Amazingly, we arrived fifteen minutes before our flight was to leave. Running down the jetway, a miracle happened. The plane was waiting for us and they gave us seating in first class. We gave thanks to God for all He had done for us and then fell asleep.

In Panama, we passed through an immigration checkpoint where I laid my passport down on a counter. I forgot it until we passed into the other part of the airport. When I realized I didn't have my passport, Barb returned to the other part of the airport to find my passport while I stayed with the luggage. I prayed Barb would return with my passport knowing God's presence was with her. When Barb arrived at the location where I had left my passport, there it was. It was another miracle from God that the passport wasn't stolen and that the officer allowed her to take it with her.

The LORD your God goes with you; he will never leave you nor forsake you. (Deuteronomy 31:6 NIV)

Honduras

We had one more nation to visit. We had received an invitation to come to Honduras and spend a weekend with the Verbo church in San Pedro Sula. It was exciting to meet this new pastor, his wife, family, and church.

Pastor Jorge Carrera met us at the airport and took us to the home of a church family where we would be staying. Jorge, a fun-loving person, was so sociable, being with him for the first time was like we had known him all his life.

That night Jorge had me preach at their Friday night meeting. After the meeting, Jorge gave me a schedule for the next day. Jorge had us meeting with different families of the church every two-and-a-half hours, starting at 8 a.m. and going until 9 p.m. At 9 p.m., we were standing at the front door of a house thinking it was another family to meet when Jorge opened the door.

When we entered Jorge's house, we asked who was next for us to meet.

Jorge said, "No one else."

I thought for a moment and said with a smile, "Gosh, Jorge, it's only 9 p.m. and I have nothing else to do for the next eight hours except sleep. Surely, you would like for me to visit another family or two."

Jorge laughed and replied "Dooonnn, No Dooonnnn."

The next morning, I preached in the church and we all had a great time. That afternoon, I participated in baptizing ten new Christians in a river not too far from the city. In the evening, I was asked to share with the young adults.

When we arrived at the church, I was dismayed to see the skimpy, tight clothes the young people were wearing. I felt the immoral appearance was an offense to the word the Holy Spirit wanted to bring to these young ones He loved so much. I began speaking about how immorality was rapidly spreading across the nations. I spoke about how it's the young people who the enemy wants to attack with immoral appearances. I shared with them how certain types of clothing should never be found on God's sons and daughters.

Hearing these words, the youth began pulling sweatshirts over their shoulders hanging down to their waistlines. Some put jackets on. The young men pulled their jeans up over their hips. Righteousness was on display. It was a beautiful thing that the Holy Spirit was doing with His loved ones.

We were taken back to Jorge's house where Jorge thanked me for being bold and sharing about morality in the church. We rested that night knowing we only spoke to the young adults that which God had put on our hearts. God was preparing us for more witnessing about God's Kingdom and His righteousness. We returned to the States to make ourselves ready for more work in India.

Chapter 11

A Change Is Coming

Therefore, my dear brothers, stand firm. Let nothing move you. Always give yourselves fully to the work of the Lord, because you know that your labor in the Lord is not in vain. (1 Corinthians 15:58 NIV)

Guatemala

Barb and I spent the next few months preparing more aid to be sent to the needy in Central America. The aid stored in our three warehouses was growing rapidly. We began to realize that our work of sending aid to those in need in far off places needed our undivided attention. Speaking it through with Joseph Anfuso we felt honored by him that he saw the need as well. A new work would be established to continue to send out this quantity of aid. The name "Gifts Of Love International" was given to this new endeavor. I traveled to Yerington to help load a container being shipped to Guatemala from the west coast. Barely having time to catch my breath, I returned home and began loading two more containers in

Wentzville. Within four days, three containers of relief aid were on their way to Guatemala.

We flew to Guatemala to help clear the containers out of customs. With Ronnie Gilmore's help, the containers were shortly released and sent to a warehouse in Guatemala City where they would be unloaded and the process of distribution began.

While distributing the aid to the churches in Guatemala City and the interior parts of the nation, I met Rafa Barrios, a pastor of a church in the small town of Cerinal, not far from Guatemala City. Previously, he was an alcoholic living on the streets of Guatemala. As he became conscious one morning, he heard a man preaching the gospel of Jesus Christ on the very street where he slept that night. As he listened to God's Word, he became convicted of his sin. He heard that Jesus suffered and died for all his sins. That morning, he gave his life to Jesus, got a Bible, and began to preach to whoever would listen. God used Rafa for His work in Cerinal. People came and filled up the pews to hear how God saved Rafa from all his troubles. Since that day, God has used Rafa to raise up more churches in the interior parts of Guatemala. I became Rafa's good friend and preached in his church and the other churches he established.

This poor man cried out, and the Lord heard him. And saved him out of all his troubles. (Psalm 34:6)

One morning, Rafa, another brother, and I met for breakfast in a quaint restaurant in Barbarena, a small town next to Cerinal. At that time, Rafa had already raised up seven churches throughout Guatemala and God was using him in a powerful way. At breakfast, I asked Rafa if he had any spiritual covering from any other group of churches or associations in or outside of Guatemala. Rafa said he did not, so I shared with him the dangers of standing alone. I saw that God was using Rafa to do His work among the poor, but without relationship and accountability to someone Rafa could trust, he was vulnerable for the enemy to try and destroy the work of God. I encouraged him to join with someone soon and submit himself to a ministry he could trust.

Rafa looked straight into my eyes and asked me to give him that spiritual covering. I told him that was not what God had called me to do, but I said I would help Rafa find a ministry that could give him the spiritual covering he needed.

Barb and I then traveled to Rafa's church and throughout the country preaching that the Kingdom of God was at hand. After several days of visiting churches, we returned to the States and began preparing for another long journey. Three weeks passed quickly and we boarded flights to India.

India

When we arrived in Hyderabad, John and Jayamani were waiting for us to pass through the airport doors. They were dressed in their beautiful Indian clothing with their wonderful smiles. They led us to their vehicle and we began the long four-hour drive to their orphanage in Jangon.

Upon arriving, we were given a room to use while in Jangon. More than 250 children lived onsite and they all participated in a drama welcoming us. They sang, danced, and wore big smiles. They were beautiful.

The next day, I was to participate in a wedding ceremony by delivering a message to the bride and groom. It was a great mystery as to what to say. The bride was a bit late arriving which gave me extra time to search the scriptures. I shared my thoughts for about twenty minutes while the bride and groom sat quietly, never taking their eyes off me. They appeared to take in every word God was speaking through me. When the ceremony ended, the celebration began. It was a time of great joy. Barb and I saw firsthand an Indian wedding. After an hour and a half of celebrations, John, Jayamani, Barb, and I returned to the orphanage.

On Sunday, I preached in a Baptist church with over 400 in attendance. We were stunned seeing the beautiful colors of the saris the women wore. From the pulpit, we could look up at the second-floor balcony. The view of all the different colors was spectacular. Finishing my message, I gave an invitation for anyone to come forward who desired to receive Jesus as Lord and Savior. Many came from each direction and invited Jesus into their hearts.

That afternoon, the four of us and our driver visited churches in several small villages. I preached in each village. After a full day of travel and preaching, we all returned to the orphanage for a night's rest.

The next day many men and women came to the orphanage to be baptized. A concrete cover was removed from the baptismal pool.

John, with other brothers, began baptizing all those who confessed Jesus Christ as Lord and Savior. After the baptisms ended, I was asked to share with their guests a word from God. In a large hall of the orphanage, the guests, workers, and children gathered together to receive God's Word.

At the end of the week, John and Jayamani drove us to the airport for our flight to Kolkata. There we met up with our friend, Rajib Arohan. We arrived midday and immediately had a meeting with the leadership of the ministry. I spoke with them about politics in the church and the joy of putting their trust in the God of creation and not in the intelligence of man.

The joy of trusting God brings new strength to one's soul.

As we have been approved by God to be entrusted with the gospel, even so we speak, not as pleasing men, but God who tests our hearts. (1 Thessalonians 2:4)

The following day, Rajib, Barb, and I traveled to a community where I preached in a small building alongside a beautiful lake with huge, overshadowing shade trees. God sent the beautiful weather for that day. The building was packed with people: standing room only. As always, at the end of the message, I gave an invitation for anyone desiring to make Jesus Christ their Lord and Savior to come forward for prayer. The front filled with people. Many received salvation, others were healed, and all received more of God. After the meeting, we enjoyed sitting by the lake under one of the tall shade trees.

After leaving that beautiful setting, we walked a long distance until we came upon a small building alongside a railroad track. Next, to the track, a couple of benches had been placed under a small roof for passengers to relax while waiting for a train. It was getting late when I asked Rajib how long we had to wait for the next train to arrive.

Rajib responded, "Don, God is good."

It was not what I was expecting to hear, but it was such a beautiful response from a servant of God who put his entire trust in our living God. I will never forget that moment in time when I needed to hear those exact words. The train arrived a short time later and we traveled for three-hours to Purulia, Rajib's hometown. Arriving at a hotel, we received a good night's rest and looked forward to Rajib's ministry plan for the day.

Rajib took us to a Leper colony in which his ministry served. The colony was in the vicinity of Purulia. Upon arriving, it was easy to see the love Rajib had for the people. Rajib kept introducing us to different people and families that were part of the colony. We went from one small house to another. I was amazed at the different types of work each one performed. There were those who worked with leather, purse makers, carvers of statues, bottle collectors, carpenters, and so many other types of activities for those who worked with their hands.

We had donated to Rajib's ministry to purchase something for the children. Rajib had used the donation to purchase a tin cup and a tin plate for each child. They had wrapped each cup and plate in a colorful gift wrap and labeled them for a certain child.

I noticed how the community all tried to eat their meals together under a canopy, but there was not enough room. I sought Rajib's advice as to the cost of building a larger concrete patio with a canopy to cover it. Rajib gave me an estimate and Barb and I were able to leave a blessing with him to do the work. We had discovered that when we helped with various needs, the joy of the Lord filled our hearts.

Do not sorrow, for the joy of the Lord is your strength. (Nehemiah 8:10)

The following morning after another good night's rest, we were on a northbound train to North Bengal. There, I had the privilege of preaching in many churches. In one particular church, there was a young woman, about twenty years old who sat on the ground in the first row directly in front of me as I preached. No matter what I said, she nodded her head in agreement. I was certain she was a Christian and had heard this teaching before. I was impressed that she seemed to really love the Lord.

When I gave an invitation to receive Jesus as Lord and Savior, she was the only one who raised her hand. As I began to lead her in prayer to give her heart to Jesus, she began to cry from her innermost being. It was the sincerest repentance I had ever witnessed. I was certain there was a huge celebration going on by angelic hosts in heavenly places. She was surely a new convert. It was a perfect ending to our time in India. The next day, we returned to Kolkata to begin our long journey home to the States.

Bus for El Salvador

While we were in India, we received a donation of a school bus to be given to a church in Central America. I sent out an e-mail announcement and within two weeks a church in El Salvador indicated they would like to be the recipient of this yellow, North American school bus.

The church pastor notified me that he and a church member would be flying to St. Louis to receive the bus and drive it back to El Salvador. Neither of them spoke a word of English, but they both wore a big smile as a result of the blessing. They came to our home for a two-day stay while preparing the bus for a three-thousand-mile journey to El Salvador. They told me they would use the bus to increase attendance at their church meetings. We prayed for them and blessed their travel. Seven days later, I heard from them that they had just arrived home. I gave thanks to God for His loving care over these two El Salvador brothers.

A Year of Travel

During the next twelve months, Barb and I continued to travel to El Salvador, Honduras, and Guatemala. When we weren't in one of these countries, we were in Yerington, NV or Elverson, PA, loading aid in containers. Frequently, we could be found working in our warehouse in Wentzville, MO. We continue to give full time to loading aid items in forty-foot containers and shipping them to Central America and India. No matter where the aid went, we followed the container to help get it released from customs and ensure its distribution.

During this work of sending aid to the poor, we would stay in the receiving countries, preaching in the churches and receiving short-term missionaries for various projects.

Teams came from Missouri, Pennsylvania, Nevada, and even Alaska. Some of these teams were serving at an orphanage called "Casa Bernabe" meaning "House of Barnabas." No matter what their mission, we were always delighted to help them with their projects. Sometimes there were evangelistic or construction projects, or they might have come to just help unload and distribute aid. It was always a pleasure for Barb and me to see people of God take seven to ten days away from their routine activities to serve the needy in a distant land.

Change Is Coming

Early one morning during our time in prayer and the Word, God told me that the task of sending physical aid to the poor had come to a close. I couldn't believe what I was hearing. I began to laugh out loud. The business of life created by the work of sending aid to the needy was about to change. I found myself happy and full of joy knowing God was bringing a new challenge to our lives.

I got up from my chair and said to Barb, "Would you like to hear what God just spoke to me?"

"Yes, of course!" said Barb. "Tell me."

"God said the season of sending physical aid to the poor has come to a close," I said and then began to cry uncontrollably.

I loved this work. I really didn't want to stop doing it. When I finally was able to stop feeling the pain of not sending aid to other nations, I felt as if someone had just removed an immense burden from my shoulders. I felt free once again. I hadn't felt such freedom for many years. We had been sending aid to the poor for more than twelve years.

To everything there is a season, A time for every purpose under heaven. (Ecclesiastes 3:1)

The first year we were involved in aid distribution, we sent out one container. Twelve years later, after sending out twenty containers during the year, our warehouses were still full of aid. I began to question if the word I had received was really from God. Then several confirmations came that the Word was from God.

The first confirmation came when one of the pastors I respected greatly, called me and asked to have some time with me. When we met the next day, he told me that he had a dream that my work of sending aid to the poor had come to an end. He also said that the money I was using to send containers would now be used to help pastors in different churches. No one except Barb knew anything about the word I had received in the living room of our home. There was no way this pastor could have known what the Lord spoke to me. God confirmed His Word to me through this man.

Another confirmation came when we were in Hershey, PA. at the National Pet Grooming Exposition. The owners of the exposition gave us a booth to raise money for our ministry work. We hadn't raised yet much when Sally and Gwen came to the booth and asked how our booth was doing. "Not so good," I told them, 'but the show wasn't over."

Sally looked straight at me and asked, "Have you ever considered that this season of work might be coming to a close?"

I looked at her thinking, *How did she know?*

A third confirmation came when we returned home from Hershey. I received a telephone call from Richard Nuti, the brother in charge of handling the containers in Yerington, NV. During the call, he told me that this would be the last time their church would be able to send aid to Guatemala. The warehouse would no longer be available to them. They now had nowhere to collect and store the aid. A few days later, I received a phone call from Paul Ranck, a brother in Elverson, PA. stating the same thing. Both brothers were concerned about telling me because they didn't want to disappoint me. Little did they know this confirmed again what God had already revealed to me.

In late August of 2005, Hurricane Katrina devastated New Orleans along with other parts of the Gulf Coast. It was one of the five deadliest hurricanes in the history of the United States. It claimed the lives of 1,833 people and left millions of others homeless. Louisiana's Emergency Response System was activated along with many relief foundations, churches, and private organizations that came to help supply the mammoth amount of aid needed. Aid would soon be sent into those areas affected by Katrina. Knowing that the Lord was their refuge, we rose to the occasion to help those victims.

I will say of the LORD, "He is my refuge and my fortress, my God, in Him I will trust." (Psalm 91:2)

We had a large warehouse in Wentzville filled with furniture, appliances, clothing, shoes, hospital equipment, toys, building materials, and miscellaneous items. I had a desire to send all the aid that was left in the warehouse to the victims of Hurricane Katrina. We began preparing wood pallets filled with relief aid. God had financially blessed us to pay for the shipments of aid. When the last container was loaded and our warehouse in Wentzville was empty, we saw the end of a season completed. We were grateful that God used us for many years to help those in need.

Don't Count Yourself Short

Several days later, I received a telephone call from Mike Stevens, a dear friend in the Chicago area. Mike was the pastor of the church where we had heard the gospel preached and gave our lives to Jesus. When I heard Mike's voice, I remembered Rafa's desire for spiritual covering.

I shared with Mike about Pastor Rafa and how he had raised up seven churches and was now looking for spiritual covering. I felt in my heart this call from Mike was not coincidental. I immediately thought that Mike was the man God was sending to give this brother a spiritual covering.

After listening to everything I had to say, Mike told me, "Don't count yourself short." "No Mike, I could never do that," I replied.

Mike repeated his words, "Don't count yourself short."

"Mike, I've never been a pastor or even an elder. How could I ever give spiritual covering to a church, much less seven churches?" I asked.

Mike replied, "I don't know, but don't count yourself short."

I came away from the phone call perplexed. I didn't know what to think. I needed time to pray and know God's will. I asked for all spiritual wisdom and understanding.

We. . .pray for you. . .to ask that you may be filled with the knowledge of his will in all wisdom and spiritual understanding. (Colossians 1:9)

After sending the last containers of relief away, I felt we needed to visit some dear friends, Memli and Luiza in Albania. They were doing great work in raising up churches throughout the interior parts of their country. The war was over and most refugee camps were disbanded. There was no longer a need to travel through Greece to enter the country. The beautiful new Tirana International Airport was open and travelers were arriving and leaving daily.

As we thought about returning to Albania, we remembered our good friend, Judy Deck, had mentioned she would like to visit one of the nations where we had previously worked. She was a men and women's hair stylist and a person who loved life and fun and exciting to be with. We invited her to go with us to Albania. She asked if her mother, Lee, could join us as well. We agreed remembering Judy's mom was a very friendly person.

Judy called us a couple nights prior to the four of us leaving to inquire if there would be much walking in Albania. I said there could be, but I thought there would be no problem hiring a taxi to take us around to the various places we wanted to visit. Judy's mom was eighty-three years old and had a problem walking from her kitchen to her bedroom at home. I thought that shouldn't be a problem using a taxi to take us from place to place.

The righteous will live by faith. (Romans 1:17 NIV)

Concerned but in faith, Lee made us a foursome. Arriving in Rome, we walked a long distance to our gate. Lee never complained about any pain. I carried all the carry-ons, piling them on top of my one roll-about. The only problem this caused was that I had to explain to each airline agent why I had so many carry-ons.

All went well and when we all arrived in Albania, we had a taxi transport us about seven city blocks to the house where we would be staying. I hired this cab to be at the same house at 9:00 a.m. each day.

The next day, we were on the street waiting for the taxi at 9:00 a.m. By 9:45 a.m., we realized the taxi was a "no-show." We decided to walk to the center of Tirana and hire a different taxi. Lee insisted on trying to walk the distance. For the next five days, Lee walked one to two miles each day. She had no complaints. She was full of gratitude to God as this gave her opportunities to share the Gospel on the streets of Tirana, Albania every day.

On the fifth day, Memli and Luiza took the four of us in a taxi to Iba, a village in the mountains where they shared in a children's work about the goodness of God. When the taxi arrived in the village, the children began to come. Upon seeing them, Lee began to cry. When asked where she was hurting, she said that she wasn't hurting. The only hurt she had was because of the poverty she saw among the children. She then walked up a long, steep hill for a short meeting with the children.

Judy and Lee stayed in Albania with us for five days, then they boarded flights to return home. Lee told us that the five days with us flew by like one. Barb and I stayed two more days in Albania and then returned home.

Four months after my conversation with Mike, Barb and I were in the hearth room of our home praying and seeking God's guidance. God spoke to me again saying I would no longer send physical aid to those as in the past, but would now begin to send spiritual aid to where He would lead me. This answered my prayers. We were to go and commit ourselves to giving spiritual covering to Rafa and the seven churches he and his team oversaw. I knew God was showing me how this spiritual covering was to function:

a. Pray for each pastor, spouse, family, and church each day.
b. Bring council, direction, and wisdom when asked for it.
c. Return to the church in a time of serious need.

I had no idea what God had planned for our lives, but I believed God would continue to show me what Barb and I should be doing. It was beyond anything I had ever hoped for. It was an incredible work that God was about to bring to us.

I pray also that the eyes of your heart may be enlightened in order that you may know the hope to which he has called you. (Ephesians 1:18-19 NIV)

I began to make plans to drive from our home in Missouri to Guatemala in early January of the next year. I felt that Barb and I would spend three months visiting churches we had been to in the past. At the end of three months, we would leave our vehicle there and begin traveling by air to and from Guatemala when needed.

Our plans were firm as we acknowledged God was leading us.

"Beautiful color of the saris."

Chapter 12

HE MADE A GATE WHERE THERE WAS NO GATE!

My God shall supply all your need according to His riches in glory by Christ Jesus. (Philippians 4:19)

Third Visit to India

It was our third visit to India and excitement was growing in our hearts for the work God had planned for us. In Kolkata, we were met by Rajib and his team. They drove us to a hotel where Rajib spoke with me about our itinerary for the next few days.

I was carrying a word in my heart for the brothers from the Holy Spirit, so I asked Rajib if I could meet with him and his team for breakfast in the morning. Rajib agreed. When we met, I told them about serving God and not man and reminded them what Paul said in 1 Corinthians 10:33, "Just as I also please all men in all things, not seeking my own profit, but the profit of many, that they may be saved." They listened intently with open minds and hearts as I encouraged them to know who they are in Christ.

Then Rajib, Barb, and I began to travel through the eastern cities of West Bengal where I shared God's Word. Rajib and his team had worked to raise up churches in these areas and God was opening doors for His gospel to reach the lost.

Our ministry had been supporting a widow and her three small children in one of the villages we visited. She was the wife of a pastor who had been murdered because of his Christian beliefs and teachings. She was hungry to hear more about the love Christ Jesus had for her and her children. Those in her village had also been taught God's Word and knew His blessings.

The following day, we went with Rajib to visit the construction site for a new building that would soon be the home of a leadership institute. The institute would train young men for the works of service in the Kingdom of God.

We continued to visit churches where I would preach and Rajib would translate. In each community, the vast number of people who came responded to the gospel without hesitation. After three days of preaching, we needed to return to Kolkata to prepare for our upcoming travel to Hyderabad. Rajib took us to the airport the next morning. We all felt our time together was too short, but our schedule didn't allow for more days in Kolkata.

When we arrived in Hyderabad, John and Jayamani met us at the airport and drove us to the orphanage where the children welcomed us with a song and a short program. I spoke briefly with the children and then we were given a very comfortable room on the second floor of the administration building.

Several months before we traveled to India the second time, we had raised enough money to buy a new bus for the orphanage. The bus was to be used to transport student nurses daily from their living quarters to the nurse's academy. It also transported twelve single ladies to the orphanage several times each week to participate in sewing classes. The ladies hoped to earn financial support for their families using the knowledge of sewing.

On our first day at the orphanage, John and Jayamani took us to a community where they were managing a children's medical clinic. Doctors and nurses had volunteered to inoculate the infants and small children against childhood diseases. The inoculations took place under a large shade tree. While the clinic was in progress, Barb and I were invited to share children's Bible stories and speak specifically about our lives. Many adults and children came and sat on the ground to listen while awaiting their turn in the clinic.

He who has pity on the poor lends to the Lord, And He will pay back what he has given. (Proverbs 19:17)

After the clinic ended, John and Jayamani led us to another area where they had raised up a ministry for the elderly. I spoke about the love God has for His people of all ages. Through God's Word, the elderly could see how their lives were enriched by the love within them for each other. Because of their age and all they experienced over many years, they were equipped to encourage and help others to know the faithfulness of God's love. I was overwhelmed by their warm hearts and desire to know more about God. We left the elderly that day knowing how much God loved the older ones.

In the days that followed, we traveled to more churches preaching God's Word. The Holy Spirit would bring revelation to me from the vivid, colorful writings of the prophets. At the end of several days, the four of us returned to the orphanage so Barb and I could prepare for our travel back to the States. Our time in India drew to a close too fast. We were becoming close to John and Jayamani. The wonderful work these two servants of God had raised up is remembered in eternity. I felt strongly about following John's lead.

Early the next morning, we left the orphanage on our way to the airport. Jayamani questioned me as to my thoughts of returning in the following year to do an evangelistic campaign. John felt that the campaign could bring more than ten thousand people to hear God's Word. He also felt that if it was successful the first year, a repeat in the second year could possibly bring more than fifty thousand people. I was overwhelmed to think that God could use me to bring thousands of people to the saving grace of Jesus Christ. We spoke all the way to the airport about the work God was doing in India and we agreed to pray about an evangelistic campaign in the upcoming year.

We arrived early and checked in at the airport. As we waited to board the flight, I thought about our days in India. Working with the leaders in two different ministries was a blessing. We encountered ministries with men who were loving and kind to each other while caring for their own flock.

We returned home in the autumn when the trees were shedding their foliage and the beauty of the season spoke of the beauty of God's ways. The leaves showed their colors before falling to the ground waiting for a new season to produce stronger, larger, and more beautiful plants. I felt much like this in my heart. I was excited about seeing our family again, but it was just like the leaves. They turn to beautiful colors then fall off only to see new ones take shape in the next season. Soon the holidays become only memories while new adventures with God were ready to unfold. Soon we would leave for another adventure in another nation.

Unless a grain of wheat falls into the earth and dies, it remains alone; but if it dies, it bears much fruit. (John 12:24) *ESVS*

Return to Guatemala

At the beginning of the year, during its coldest season, Barb and I left Missouri driving south through Mexico on our way to Guatemala. Three hundred miles south of our home, we encountered rain, sleet, and ice on the turnpike. I slowed the Blazer down to almost a crawl. It wasn't long before we came upon a terrible accident bringing traffic to a stop. A horse trailer was laying on its side. No one seemed to be hurt and the horses seemed fine as they stood on the shoulder of the highway.

We continued on through Oklahoma and Texas and arrived at the Mexican border two days later. We worked with the Mexican customs and immigration officials to get our paperwork in order.

Then we stayed that night in a hotel in Matamoros, a Mexican border town. Early Saturday morning, we were on our way to Tampico, 250 miles south of the U.S. border. I was to teach that evening at a leadership meeting and preach the next morning in the church.

Upon arriving about 2:00 p.m. in Tampico, brothers met us and directed us to a hotel near the church. At the hotel, I decided to remove the front license plate from the Blazer to prevent losing both plates. It seemed as though USA plates were in demand. While trying to cut the plastic lock off a new toolbox I had just purchased, the knife accidentally slipped and cut deep into my wrist. I ran to the front of the building to show Barb. The blood was gushing out of my wrist and a woman at her tienda (tiny store) pulled me inside and pushed cotton into the wound. She then called for an ambulance. It all happened so fast I had no time to reject anything taking place. Upon arriving at the hospital, a plastic surgeon was called to the scene. He told me I would undergo a thirty-minute surgery and gave me the option of putting me to sleep or just giving me a local anesthetic. I asked the doctor if I would be able to preach that evening if I was put to sleep.

The surgeon replied, "No, you will be asleep until morning."

Desiring to teach that night, I chose the local. Being awake during the operation caused me incredible pain. A nurse at my side encouraged me to keep my eyes closed. I remember my legs kept coming up off the operating table during the surgery because of the pain. The surgery lasted four and a half hours. It was music to my ears when the surgeon said he was finished.

I asked if I would be able to teach my session that night and the doctor said yes. However, twenty minutes later in recovery, I began to feel sick and vomited. That ended the possibility of my teaching. Pastor Juan Manuel drove Barb and me back to our hotel. Barb needed to help me with everything. My wrist and left arm were wrapped up in so many bandages that I couldn't get any clothes on over it. Barb had to cut a slit in the left sleeve of each of my shirts.

Sunday morning, I preached with my arm in a sling. I thought it made a great podium for holding my Bible directly in front of me. I preached for forty-five minutes, but then my arm began to swell, bringing more pain. I was then cautioned to be careful not to overdo.

On Monday morning, Pastor Juan took Barb and me to visit the surgeon. Examining the incision, we received a good report, so I decided I wanted to travel south that day to Poza Rica. However, the brothers insisted we stay two or three more days in Tampico or let someone else drive. Since it was my desire to stay on schedule, I submitted to the brothers' counsel to have someone else drive.

It is not good to have zeal without knowledge, nor to be hasty and miss the way. (Proverbs 19:2 NIV)

Pastor Juan's advice was for us to rest that night in Poza Rica. He also wanted me to meet with the church leadership there. I agreed and we were on our way with a driver Pastor Juan had found for us. In Poza Rica, a gathering of some enthusiastic leaders came to the pastor's home to listen as I shared thoughts on the indwelling of the Holy Spirit and commended the brothers with the Word of God's grace.

Early the next morning, we thanked the brothers in Poza Rica for their hospitality and continued traveling south. After our driver had driven nearly four hours, I felt he needed to return to Tampico, so I tested my driving skills with my left arm in a sling. I felt I could drive without a problem. We thanked the brother for the kindness he'd shown us in doing the driving. We blessed him and sent him on a bus back to Tampico. Once again, I was driving. The sun was setting as we arrived at a hotel two hours south of Vera Cruz. We took advantage of being on schedule and took a whole day and two nights to rest at the hotel.

Early the second morning with darkness all around, we set off from the hotel trusting God with our travel plans. Driving south, we watched the sun begin to rise in the east. The scenery was breathtaking with its majestic mountains and natives dressed in their colorful attire. I was thankful to God for these blessings of adventure.

About 2:00 p.m., we arrived in Tuxtla Gutierrez, a town high up in the mountains of southern Mexico. It was a thriving, bustling city with many vehicles on the highway traveling north and south. Soon a hotel was in sight. As I pulled into the parking lot, I whispered a prayer to obtain a nice clean room.

I was pleased when the attendant at the reception desk assigned us a room overlooking the street. Looking out the window, I could see the way we would be heading in the morning. We had dinner in the hotel restaurant while watching the darkness creep in. Early in the morning, we drove south again.

A new expressway was being built south of Tuxtla Gutierrez creating many detours. Only a single lane of traffic going south was permitted. Driving in the darkness of early morning hours brought feelings of insecurity. We prayed for God's peace and protection.

After several hours of driving, we were within twenty minutes of the Guatemalan border. I attempted to pass a small truck, but as I came alongside the pickup, the driver turned quickly to the left causing me to swerve onto a very narrow shoulder. As I tried to slow down, the left front tire dropped off the shoulder causing the vehicle to go out of control and down a steep embankment. I saw a huge tree looming directly in front of the Blazer. I knew if we hit the tree, both us could be killed. I did my best to go around the tree while preventing the vehicle from overturning. Miraculously, I missed the tree and kept the vehicle on all four wheels.

"Not by might nor by power, but by My Spirit," says the LORD of hosts. (Zechariah 4:6)

I had no seat belt on because my arm was in a sling. The vehicle went through a barbed wire fence, knocking down a concrete fence post and coming to a jolting stop. I was knocked unconscious when my head hit the windshield. When I regained consciousness, I was in front of Barb on the passenger side of the Blazer. Through all the luggage and personal belongings that flew forward, I worked to get back behind the steering wheel.

Then I heard a man with perfect English yell, "Sir, are you alright?"

"Yes, I think so," I replied.

I saw about five men running down the steep embankment.

"How is the lady with you?" asked the man with perfect English.

"I think I'm fine," Barb replied.

The English-speaking man said, "Sir, you need to get your vehicle out of here because if the police come you will be in a lot of trouble."

I asked, "How do I get out of here?"

The man said, "Just follow me."

It appeared there was no way out. Our vehicle was on the inside of the fenced area and the English-speaking man was on the outside of the fence. The man began to run along the fence and told me to follow him. I put the Blazer in four-wheel drive and followed. After going a couple hundred feet, I saw what appeared to be an open gate in the fence.

I yelled at the man who had just passed the open gate, "Can I go through this gate?"

The man yelled, "Where? I see no gate."

I yelled back, "It's right in front of me and it's open."

Again the man said, "There is no gate there."

I yelled back, "Yes, there is."

"Well, go through it," said the man.

I turned the wheel to the left, went through the gate, and directly up the embankment. Our vehicle was once again on top of the highway.

God, who gives life to the dead and calls those things which do not exist as though they did. (Romans 4:17)

I never looked back to see if there really was a gate because at that moment in time it didn't seem to matter. Later, I came to the conclusion that there was never a gate there because the fence was at the bottom of the steep embankment and there would have been no reason or room for a gate. All things being possible with God, I knew that God made a way for Barb and me when there seemed to be no way.

I crossed over the vacated highway with our limping vehicle to get to a small shop. I stepped out of the vehicle and walked around it to assess the damage. All four tires were flat and the right front wheel was bent in and up under the vehicle.

I asked Barb to go in the tienda and inquire if they had a phone she could use. When she tried to get out of the vehicle she dropped to the ground because of excruciating pain below her stomach. Four men near the tienda gently lifted her back into the vehicle. She was crying because of the pain. I went into the tienda requesting to use a telephone, but the attendant would not allow it.

I left the tienda and coaxed the Blazer with its four flat tires, across the highway to a small tire repair shop. There I was allowed to use a telephone. The man with perfect English stayed with me until I was able to talk with my friend, Mariano. Just like the gate where there was no gate, I didn't know who the man was with perfect English nor where the other men that I saw run down the embankment came from.

Mariano had come to the border to help me get the vehicle licensed to drive in Guatemala. He knew nothing about the accident. When I told him about the terrible predicament we were in, Mariano and his friend, Augusto, came right away to the tire repair shop. They immediately picked Barb up and put her in the front passenger seat of Mariano's car. There were no medical facilities within one hundred miles. After the tires were repaired, I paid the bill and we headed to the border. I drove Mariano's car and Mariano drove my limping vehicle. At the border, I found much grace from the control officers. They allowed Mariano and me to pass through without any hassle.

Driving in Guatemala for just a short distance, we realized we couldn't continue at that slow pace for the next one hundred miles. We stopped and prayed to find a tow truck for hire. We continued only a short distance and there was a sign in the window of a tow truck on the side of the highway that said, "For Hire." The truck wasn't much to look at, but the Blazer needed help to go any farther. We hired the owner of the truck to tow my vehicle more than one hundred miles to a repair shop in Huehuetenango. The owner of the truck charged me only one hundred dollars for all his time, labor, and expenses. Three and a half hours later, we pulled into a repair shop in Huehuetenango.

We were then taken to the public hospital for x-rays and observation. We stayed with the pastor of the church and his wife whom I had worked with in the past. Barb was in a wheelchair for two weeks because it was too painful for her to walk. We spent those two weeks recuperating and pondering the word in our hearts that

God gave us in the hearth room of our home more than a month ago. I continued to seek God's direction knowing that the enemy was doing all he could to try and stop us from doing God's work.

We were on the mend and walking with nearly no pain. We left Huehuetenango and began traveling to churches throughout the interior parts of the country. We would spend three days and three nights at each church we visited and would bring several teachings to the congregations. We had great times with the pastors, families, and churches.

Time passed quickly and we moved on to work with churches in and around the Capitol City. My friend, Bill Gorrell, from the United States, came to Guatemala to work with me. On one particular Saturday night, Barb, Bill, and I were to preach in Rafa's church in Cerinal. I asked Bill to bring the word.

After a great time of worship, Bill went on the platform and began to preach. He spoke with great authority for about forty-five minutes. At the end of his message, he gave the microphone to me and asked me to bring a closing word to the meeting. Rafa, the pastor of the church, was on the platform with Bill.

The people were standing and as I took the microphone, the Holy Spirit said, "Have the people move into the center aisle."

So I instructed the people to move into the center aisle.

Then the Holy Spirit said, "Have all the people raise their hands unto the Lord."

I had the people raise their hands unto the Lord.

The Holy Spirit then said, "Now have the people wave their hands and arms to God."

I followed suit and asked the people to wave their hands and arms unto our God. The people began doing as I did. While worshiping the Lord, people in the back of the church began falling to the floor under the power of the Holy Spirit without anyone praying for them. No one was touching them. Only the presence of God was upon them. As people were falling in the back of the church, the same thing was happening in the center aisle and working its way to the front. People were on the floor. By the power of the Holy Spirit, God's people were touched, healed, and set free from demonic oppression. Rafa looked bewildered, proclaiming he never saw anything like this before. The music was loud, some of the people were crying, others laughing, but most were on the floor. God was on the move in that small building.

At the end of the meeting, I asked Rafa if he had ever received the fullness of the Holy Spirit in his life. Rafa wasn't sure what I was asking. So, I made plans to meet with Rafa's pastors on the upcoming Tuesday, to speak on living in the fullness of the Holy Spirit.

On Tuesday morning, I arrived at the church in Cerinal to speak about the Holy Spirit. By the end of the meeting, the pastors and their wives were crying out for their lives to be filled up with the fullness of God's Holy Spirit. They were on their knees praying in tongues and prophesying.

When Paul had laid hands on them, the Holy Spirit came upon them, and they spoke with tongues and prophesied. (Acts 19:6)

It was a new dawning for us. A new season had begun. Neither of us had ever asked God for a ministry working with pastors, but now it seemed He wanted us to help them reach the calling that God had placed upon them. I knew we needed God to do what He had given us to do. Our own skills wouldn't work anymore. Only through God's Holy Spirit would Barb and I be able to reach the new heights that God placed before us.

"Don preaching during a medical clinic in India."

Chapter 13

CALLED TO PREACH

Listen closely to my words. Do not let them out of your sight, keep them within your heart; for they are life to those who find them and health to a man's whole body. (Proverbs 4:20-22 NIV)

Adventures in Guatemala

I felt a new excitement since the night the Holy Spirit fell on God's people in the small church in Cerinal, Guatemala. Real needs were met and revelation of my life's purpose was revealed. The revelation that my work belonged to the Holy Spirit was intensified. All I needed to do was believe.

Rafa had invited me to come with him and two of his pastors to a location in a densely wooded area of Guatemala. The only passage to the village was navigating up the river Rio Negro. I was excited about this new adventure. I invited my friend and translator, Pablo, to come along for the adventure.

Pablo and his wife Nancy traveled with Barb and me through the mountains to a small town where Barb and Nancy would wait for Pablo and me to return from our one-day mission trip. After Pablo and I met with Rafa and his pastors, Edgar and Hector, we traveled many hours through small rivers, wooded areas, and small villages to a huge river passage. There we boarded a small boat to take us up the river, passing many coves and tributaries before arriving at a small Indian village. That afternoon, I had the joy of preaching God's Word to the indigenous people.

A young missionary priest was one of those attending the meeting. He wore his black clothes with his white collar. As I preached, the young priest appeared very upset with my message. At the end of the meeting, he asked me if we could talk in private. Concerned, I went with the young man who asked questions about my faith in Christ Jesus. As I began to speak, I knew the guidance of God's presence. I felt peace coming over this young man's life. I desired to bring truth concerning uncertainties of salvation this man had in his heart and mind. When my time of bringing God's peace into this seeker's life ended, the young man expressed his gratefulness for the time I spent with him.

If you abide in My word, you are My disciples indeed. And you shall know the truth, and the truth shall make you free. (John 8:31)

At lunchtime, the women of the village brought out a large pot of hot broth with fish heads floating in it. I didn't feel I should test God at this moment, so I graciously passed on that lunch. However, Pablo enjoyed the broth.

It wasn't long before we headed back down the river. All five of us boarded the small boat. It was late in the day and the boat was moving fast downstream. After half the time it took going upstream, we arrived at our vehicles and traveled back to where Barb and Nancy were waiting. It wasn't long before the lunch proved disastrous for Pablo. He felt terrible and ended up spending much of the night in the bathroom. When morning came, Pablo only wanted to go home!

Mike and Penny

When the four of us returned to the Capitol City, Pablo and Nancy headed home while Barb and I prepared to receive our special friends, Mike and Penny. We invited them to come to Guatemala and travel with us among the churches. Mike was also going to teach some of the sessions at the two-day conferences scheduled in a couple of days for the seven churches belonging to Rafa's organization.

Mike and Penny arrived late in the day, so they went straight to the hotel to get some rest and be ready for their packed agenda the next morning. Mike was pleased with all my plans for the four of us.

On the first morning of their new experience, the four of us met for a great Guatemalan buffet breakfast at the hotel restaurant. My prayers and thoughts were on the miles of highways I would be driving over the next few days.

After breakfast, our first stop was San Juan Ostuncalco, a small town high in the mountains of Guatemala. Residents boast of the snow they receive in the cold winter months, but we had only observed heavy frost on the ground in early morning hours.

Mike and I were looking forward to the meetings at two churches in the mountainous regions of Guatemala. Mike had three meetings and I was involved in two. We spent much time seeking God's presence for the people we were ministering to over the next two days.

Sunday night our weekend ended. On Monday morning, we left San Juan and drove from the high mountainous altitudes to the lower coastal highways where temperatures were much more agreeable. Several hours later, we passed through the large thriving industrial city of Escuintla. Leaving the city, we drove on long stretches of straight highway through many miles of sugarcane country.

As we were traveling through this section, Mike asked me a question, "Where do you want to build your base for the work God is giving you?"

I was surprised because up until now, Mike knew nothing about what God spoke to Barb and me concerning our upcoming work. Not only did Mike not know anything about our intended work, but the area we were passing through was exactly where we were hoping to purchase land.

When I shared with Mike this was where we wanted to buy land and build our base, Mike suggested, "Let's stop and pray and ask God to open this land purchase right here."

I pulled the car over and we began to pray. When the prayer ended, I believed we had just touched Heaven.

This is the confidence that we have in Him: that if we ask anything according to his will, He hears us. And if we know that He hears us—whatever we ask—we know that we have the petitions that we asked of Him. (1 John 5:14-15)

After our time of prayer, I drove to the location where we would teach in a two-day conference with pastors and their wives. These were the men and women Rafa had discipled to build churches in the interior parts of Guatemala. We were in a small community called "Los Esclavos" which means, "The Slaves." Our teachings on the Kingdom of God brought much blessing and direction to these pastors and their churches. The pastors discovered stronger foundations of righteousness and purity for their church.

When the conference ended, we traveled back to the hotel we stayed at when Mike and Penny first arrived in Guatemala. During the following week, we took Mike and Penny to the children's project where Barb and I were working with a ministry caring for needy little ones. Mike and Penny brought candy for the children and Mike enjoyed throwing some in the air for the children to grab.

By the end of the week, I had introduced Mike and Penny to more pastors and their wives from churches Barb and I had met while distributing aid. Mike taught in a church on the northern outskirts of the Capitol City. Near the end of his message, he went into the congregation to pray and lay hands on a married couple. As he did, the people came under the ministry of the Holy Spirit. They began to fall on their knees crying, weeping, and sobbing while calling out to God for more of Him in their lives. We witnessed many such incidences throughout the churches we visited.

It was quite evident the Holy Spirit was not only ministering to the people in the congregations, but also to Mike, Penny, Barb, and me. Without question, the four of us were feeling we needed more of God and less of ourselves. The past few days had shed new light on our hunger for the Lord. The time for us all to return home arrived quickly.

Who Will Go?

Mike and Penny lived in Kansas City, Missouri. On their way to Chicago to visit their family, they passed through St. Louis. I invited them to stay the night so Barb and I could bless them as we sat and shared life together. I told Mike that brothers from India had given Barb and me an invitation to come and conduct evangelistic outreaches, but I was unsure if this was from the Lord.

Mike responded, "If you don't go who will?"

I thought, *Yes, Lord, if I don't go, who will?* Through Mike's encouragement, I knew this challenge was from the Lord. So, we prepared our hearts, prayed, and fasted, and set our agenda and looked to God for direction.

The months that followed were filled with anticipation. Everywhere I went, thoughts of India went with me. It was God's calling going deep into my soul. I wanted to scream from the rooftop while waiting for what lay ahead. The day finally came when Barb and I boarded our flight on our way to India. Fear tried to attack me saying I wasn't qualified, I didn't know the Word well enough, and I wasn't holy enough. Each time fear came, I rejected it. I knew I wasn't qualified, but I also knew who God was and that God was with me. Even though I didn't know the Word well enough, I knew God did. I kept believing I was ready because I knew God was in me, had called me, and His hands were upon me. I continued to recite God's Word which brought me victory.

> *Listen closely to my words. Do not let them out of your sight, keep them within your heart; for they are life to those who find them and health to a man's whole body.* (Proverbs 4:20 NIV)

As we were on the last leg of our flight going into Kolkata, I was trying to stay calm while remembering all God had put on my heart for India. Rajib and some brothers met us as we were collecting our luggage. The brothers took us to a nearby hotel where we rested the night and received our itinerary for the next several days. I felt blessed to be with these men of God.

Sunday morning, I preached in one of the churches Rajib and his team founded. I preached again that evening which brought to memory the first time I had preached in a church in Kolkata and was asked to remove my shoes before walking to the pulpit. Though it was a bit uncomfortable, I had honored the men I was with by doing as they asked.

The next day, we began a long drive to our first evangelistic outreach. By the time we arrived, it was too late in the day to begin our first meeting. Also, before acquiring a hotel room Barb and I needed to sign in at the official immigration office in that city. It was the law and we needed to comply.

On the first day of the evangelistic outreach, many people attended. At first, it appeared that hundreds had come, but later it was evident that more than 2,000 people were in attendance. I preached and Rajib translated. At the end of the first meeting, hundreds came forward when the invitation was given to receive Jesus Christ as their Lord and Savior. Each one that came repeated the corporate prayer I led them in as they gave their lives to their new master. Many also came for healings as Barb and I prayed a corporate prayer for healing over them.

I am the LORD, who heals you. (Exodus 15:26)

The evangelistic meetings over the next three days were conducted the same as on the first day. Each day, the team went to a new location where a one-day evangelistic outreach was held. During those four days of meetings in four different locations, more than 10,000 people attended and hundreds gave their lives to Jesus.

On the last day of the week, Rajib, Barb, and I returned to Kolkata. On Saturday, I taught in three, one-hour sessions, and gave an opportunity to have a question and answer period. The teaching was held in a large church in Kolkata that was full of pastors, leaders, and their wives from several different churches.

The day before we were to leave Kolkata, we spent time visiting with Rajib and Subi. Our visit with these two friends seemed too short, but it had to come to an end. We said our goodbyes to Rajib and Subi and left for Hyderabad the next morning. There we met up with John and Jayamani Kolluri and traveled to Jangon where the orphanage was located. No matter the direction of travel, the larger vehicle took precedent of who had the right to the one lane highway. It was a treacherous four and half hours!

As the gates of the orphanage opened, 250 children were singing and welcoming us back to India. They sang while standing in organized lines stretching from the gates to the administration building. We were asked to share a short word as a kind gesture towards the children before we went to our sleeping quarters.

After breakfast the following morning, Jayamani showed us their elementary school with 450 students, wearing well-kept school uniforms. She also took us to the high school, introducing us to 200 teenagers ranging in age from fourteen to eighteen. Lastly, we visited a sewing class, where young and middle-aged women were learning a new profession.

John and Jayamani were two amazing people with great administrative talent. I learned to stay in a ready mode working with John because at any moment he would call on me to speak, often without any advance notice.

Preach the word! Be ready in season and out of season. (2 Timothy 4:2)

The Warangal Conferences

In the middle of the week, the four of us traveled to Warangal, the location of a three-day pastoral conference and then a four-night evangelistic crusade. I spoke each day in the conference which began with 150 pastors and their wives. By the last day of the conference, more than 400 pastors and their wives were in attendance.

Saturday morning, the last day of the conference, the pastors and their wives came to hear God's Word. I knew that God was speaking to each one in different ways. At the end of my teaching, John gave an invitation for pastors to come forward to enable Barb and me to minister to them. The line extended to the back of the building.

That evening about 2,500 people descended upon Warangal, the opening night of the evangelistic campaign. I preached on "The Abundant Life of Knowing Jesus." When I gave an invitation for people to receive Jesus as their Lord and Savior, hundreds came running to the platform. I thought they might knock it down. I later asked John if a rope could be strung up about ten feet away from the platform to prevent an accident on the platform.

There was one middle-aged man who came quickly up front. I saw him and began to proclaim the name of Jesus over his life. The instant I mentioned the name of Jesus, the man became violent. His arms were flying and he was yelling words I didn't understand. After a few minutes, he settled down and seemed to be calm. I again proclaimed the name of Jesus over him and again he got violent. I wouldn't accept this and kept proclaiming the name of Jesus. He continued this action as long as I continued proclaiming the name of the Lord. After a long time of violent reaction, he went limp.

Then I proclaimed the name of Jesus to this man and he lifted his hands and surrendered his life to our Lord. It appeared that a true victory was won that night over his life.

The second night of the campaign brought an even greater possibility of additional souls for Christ Jesus with more than 4,000 people in attendance. Again, hundreds responded to God's word and received Christ Jesus as Lord of their life. I spoke on "Coming to Our Senses." A yellow rope was hung ten feet in circumference around the platform, but the rope brought no security or safety to the platform, for when the invitation was given the ushers removed the rope and hundreds came running to the platform.

Directly in front of me was the same man who was set free the night before. As he stood there, I began to proclaim God's name over his life again. This time he showed no violence. I was so blessed to see what appeared to be total surrender. He only raised his hands to the Lord and began to worship Him.

> *If anyone is in Christ, he is a new creation; old things have passed away; behold, all things have become new.* (2 Corinthians 5:17)

The third night of the evangelistic campaign was only a couple of hours away and I knew I needed God. The first two nights were wonderful, but this was a new night and I was emotional before the Lord. When we arrived at the site of the outreach, I looked around and saw thousands of people coming through the gates. I had tears in my eyes, amazed that God would give me the right and privilege to share His Word with His people. The word I shared that night was entitled "The Love of Knowing Jesus." Over 5,500 people attended the campaign and nearly 1,000 souls received Christ Jesus as Lord and Savior.

Then came the last night of the campaign and our time in India was about to end. It was a wonderful experience being in the presence of God every day of the conference and campaign. It was difficult to think of leaving.

Sunday morning I was asked to preach in three different churches that day. The first church meeting was at 9:00 a.m. It was a Pentecostal Church that was filled to capacity. I was preaching on "Slaying Your Giant." I stacked two chairs on top of a wobbly table and climbed on top of the table. I got to the part of the battle where David asked, "Who is this uncircumcised Philistine that he should defy the armies of the living God?" I climbed up on the two folding chairs on top of the wobbly table and stood up straight. My desire was for the people to recognize this task for David was huge. I did pray diligently to not fall or have the chairs or table collapse under me. All went well and at the end of the meeting, I gave an invitation for anyone who wanted to invite Jesus into their lives to come up front. The front of the church filled with people. There were more than twenty-five people that came forward to receive Jesus. That meeting ended with great excitement. Then we were driven to the next meeting.

The next one was at 11:00 a.m. and the last meeting was at 1:00 p.m. I preached the same message in all three meetings. Each meeting brought its own responses. By the end of the third meeting,

I was exhausted, so we went back to the hotel to rest until it was time to go to the evening campaign meeting.

It was estimated more than 10,000 people attended that meeting. I preached on, "The Consequences of Sin." As it happened in preceding nights, when I gave an invitation for people to receive Christ into their lives, people came running to the platform. They wanted to be first in line to receive Christ. More than 1,300 people came forward to receive their new life in Christ.

There was one man who came forward to receive Jesus during the first meeting on Sunday at the Pentecostal church. I had just met this man a few minutes after the evening meeting ended. He was a nice-looking man in his mid-thirties dressed in all white. He was invited by John to come and give his testimony of what happened to him earlier in the day. He took the microphone and shared that he was walking past the church building earlier that morning and heard his name, David, coming from inside the building. He stepped in to hear why his name was mentioned. He stood there and listened. When he heard the invitation to surrender his life to Christ, he went forward and did just that.

He then testified that he was on his way to commit suicide. He was tired of living and was going to do away with his life, but instead of killing his body, he put to death his old lifestyle, dying unto himself.

> *I have been crucified with Christ. It is no longer I who live, but Christ lives in me and the life which I now live in the flesh I live by faith in the Son of God.* (Galatians 2:20)

At each campaign meeting with Rajib and later with John and Jayamani, many healings took place. Barb and I prayed for thousands of God's people to be healed. I had each son or daughter of our King place their hands over that part of their body that they were asking for healing as we prayed. Many testified of the healing they received.

On the last night of the campaign, I also gave an invitation for young people who wanted to give their life to full-time work in the Kingdom of God to come forward. More than fifty young adults over eighteen years of age committed to this calling.

I was so grateful to God for what had taken place during those two weeks in India.

The time in India was complete and we would rest from our work and look to God for His new direction. I realized our new calling had just begun. God was about to open a whole new work for us. It was far beyond anything we ever anticipated. The victories of the future battles became testimonies that God was the victor and anyone who joined God in these new ventures would be victors as well.

Chapter 14

HELP FOR THE ABUSED

I command you today to love the LORD your God, to walk in his ways and to keep his commands, decrees and laws; then you will live and increase, and the LORD your God will bless you in the land you are entering to possess. (Deuteronomy 30:16 NIV)

Several years ago, when Barb and I traveled in Zimbabwe, Zambia and The Congo with Richard Bartropp, God gave me the opportunity to be His witness among the poorest people I ever met. Over several years, my good friend Ramson Mumba from Zambia communicated with me and frequently invited us to come and share God's Word in the Copper Belt. With new revelation in our hearts, we prepared an itinerary for our return to Zambia.

It was mid-summer when we landed in Lusaka. Ramson and Mercy Mumba welcomed us at the airport and escorted us to our first meeting in the capital city of Lusaka. We were excited to again be among people who loved the Lord and worshiped God with all their might.

On the way to the first meeting of the conference, Ramson asked me, "What title should I use to introduce you to the people?"

I replied, "I don't know. I've never been into titles."

Ramson and Mercy laughed and Ramson responded, "No, my Brother, how may I introduce you?"

"I don't know. Honestly, I've never thought about it before," I answered.

When Ramson asked again, I finally said, "Okay, introduce me as a servant of the Lord."

Therefore, from that time forward Ramson introduced me as a servant of the Lord.

All day Saturday and Sunday morning, I had the privilege of preaching God's Word. An awesome time of praise and worship took place as I watched surrendered hands being raised unto the Lord and tears running down faces. During the following two days, Barb and I had time to rest while traveling to the Copper Belt. I used the time to prepare for the conference meetings that would take place at the end of the week.

The conference would last for several days with three sessions each day. Ramson was the overseer and was kind in giving me the majority of the sessions. Each day more people came and many responded positively to God's Word.

During one of the sessions, something happened that brought added vision to our ministry. We saw a young child bounced down on a chair caused by the forceful hand of an adult. We couldn't believe it. We carried it in our hearts but spoke very little about it to each other. Later in the day, an elderly lady came to us with a small note she had rolled up in a tiny ball. She handed it to me and asked if we would read it when we had time.

"Of course," we replied and I dropped the small roll of paper in my left shirt pocket.

I went on to speak at the last session. Though my heart was hurting because of what we had witnessed that morning, I spoke the truth with grace to those assembled. By 7:00 p.m., the sun had set. No more meetings were held because there was no light on the property. We were escorted back to the hotel to rest for the night.

We still felt stressed recalling our experience that morning. As I took everything out of my pockets, I felt the small, rolled up lump of paper. When I took it out, I remembered the elderly lady asking us to read the note when we had time.

I unrolled the piece of paper and read, "Dear Brother Don, This morning at the end of the meeting when a man was pushing that small boy, that child is my son. The man was trying to make him talk. My son has not spoken anything since the day he was born. Please pray that my son might speak."

After reading this note, we sat on the edge of our bed and began to weep. I turned on the television hoping to get my mind off the incident. A true story movie was just beginning. It was an autobiography of two women, Yvonne Fedderson and Sara O'Meara, who had been in Japan during the war entertaining the troops at Christmas. They were both professional singers and dancers.

One night while entertaining the troops, the sky opened and a torrential rain poured on the show. Everyone ran for cover. The two ladies jumped into a taxi to return to their hotel. On the way there, they saw some small orphan children standing on the street corner holding small pieces of cardboard over their heads. The children wore sparse clothes with only ragged shorts and a few torn shirts. Yvonne and Sara had the taxi stop and the two of them jumped out, grabbed the eleven children, and put them in the taxi. They took them to the hotel, quietly escorted them up to their room, and cared for them until the end of their stay in Japan. Before leaving Japan, they found a home for all the children.

When the two entertainers returned to the states, they decided to begin a new work of caring for abused children. Yvonne and Sara purchased land in the central United States, developed a farm, and used animals for child therapy. The farm had a big red barn with a white fence resembling a children's storybook farm.

"For the Love of a Child" portrayed the true story of one small child, Jacob, who had an abusive father. Jacob came to the farm after much suffering due to his father's ill-treatment. When Jacob arrived, he had a burn mark on his back the shape and size of an iron. Jacob lived there and was shown the love he had never experienced. In the eyes of the teachers, he could do no wrong.

One day when Jacob came to the dining table that was set with food and drink, he grabbed the tablecloth and yanked it as hard as he could. Food, drinks, glasses, plates, and utensils flew everywhere. Teri, one of the founders, took Jacob and while hugging and loving him, explained why what he did was wrong. For the rest of the meal, Jacob sat on her lap and ate his food. During the first three months at the farm, Jacob had not spoken a word to anyone.

One day, the director took Jacob to the barnyard. There Jacob sat on his lap as they looked upon a brown and white cow with curly white hair on its face. The cow was about thirty feet away. The director told Jacob the cow's name was Betsy. He told Jacob that if he wanted to own Betsy he could have her, but he needed to take care of her. Jacob slipped off the director's lap and walked over to the lovable, gentle cow. Jacob began to stroke Betsy's hair. He petted the cow working his way from the right side of the cow to the cow's face. He then moved all the way to the other side of Betsy. When he saw a big, bad scar on her other side he immediately stepped back. He went over to the director and wanted nothing to do with Betsy.

Again sitting on the director's lap, the director told the boy, "Jacob, when you first came to us, you had a big, bad burn on your back. But we wanted to take care of you no matter how bad your scar looked. Betsy is just like you. She also was burned bad on her side. You don't need to own Betsy or take care of her if you don't want to, it's your decision."

Jacob slid off the director's lap and walked back to Betsy and began to pet her again. The director heard Jacob talking to Betsy. For the first time in three months, Jacob talked and Betsy became his cow and friend.

All things are possible to him who believes. (Mark 9:23)

One evening after several weeks had passed, Jacob was missing and no one could find him. Then someone looked in the barn where Betsy slept. There was Jacob, all curled up sleeping in the stall with Betsy.

The movie ended with a documentary about the ministry. Jacob Fletcher portrayed Mathew Knight's life as the hurting child. As Mathew grew into adulthood, he later became the director of that orphanage. The movie depicted the life of hurting boys and girls before they came to the farm and how their lives were transformed at the farm. The orphanage grew and multiplied, opening more locations around the United States.

We sat on the edge of our bed weeping. We asked God what all these things we saw were supposed to mean to us. It was then that God put on our hearts the challenge of going home and building a program for abused children.

The next day, Ramson and Mercy drove us to Lusaka for our flight home. On the flight, I inquired of the Lord as to how we were to start this children's program. We had no experience working with hurting children and we had no money to develop the program. We had no idea where to begin in undertaking such a large task. We knew God had it all worked out. We only needed to wait upon Him. I remembered we were already working with abused children in Guatemala and believed God was going to expand that work.

A few days after arriving home, we desired to return to Guatemala. With the word God had given us in Africa, we were on the lookout for property for the project. To begin, we visited the area where many children were in need. It was near Guatemala City and children were living on dirt streets with no resemblance to any kind of family life. Barb and I had partnered with a ministry that was working with the children to give them food every Monday, Wednesday, and Saturday. This ministry played games with the children and read Bible stories to them. We jumped in and served alongside the leaders. We shared God's Word and trusted in Him to provide all that was financially needed to pay for the project and vision that would hold this work together.

I was excited God had sent us to look for property and to prepare a program to help hurting children. I wasn't worried about money. I believed everything we needed would be provided if it really was God leading us. We drove to many areas hoping to find the piece of property that God had for us. After two weeks of searching, we were still undecided. We found nothing that seemed to fit our vision. So, we took a break and returned home.

We decided to rest and wait upon God to show us the next step.

At home, we enjoyed working on the lawn and flower garden. One day, my phone rang as I sat on a boulder wall taking a break. The call was from Javier, a young man whom we enjoyed working with in Guatemala. I immediately sensed Javier's joy concerning good news for the ministry.

Javier and his wife, Mariela, had been on the lookout for land for the children's ministry. They had located 26.5 acres of land for sale near a village in Guatemala named Brito. Javier and Mariela believed the land could be what we were looking for to serve the poor.

A few days later, we were on our way to Guatemala. Arriving at the gate in the Houston airport, we heard our names come across the loudspeakers asking us to come to the gate check-in desk. An upgrade was awaiting us on our flight to Guatemala. We were treated as royalty. The meal was delicious and the seats were comfortable. Our flight was a blessing from the One who had arranged it.

Javier and Mariela met us at the airport and shuttled us to a nearby hotel. Looking out of the eleventh-floor window of our room, Barb saw the monstrous traffic on the streets of Guatemala. With all the traffic, we decided it was too late in the day to make the hour-and-a-half journey to Brito. We decided to wait until morning to travel out of the city.

The hotel accommodations and the breakfast were more than we had expected. After breakfast, we met Javier in the hotel lobby. He drove patiently through early morning rush-hour traffic for more than an hour-and-a-half. Finally, we passed through Escuintla, the industrial city twenty minutes north of Brito. The highway on the outskirts of Escuintla was in good shape. After arriving in the village of Brito, Javier announced that it was only a few more minutes to the property.

The property was beautiful! The shadow from some of the fruit trees over the land made it seem so peaceful. We began to walk to the back of the property. From the entrance to its farthest corner, it was about a quarter of a mile. I was more impressed with every step I took. We saw nearly 150 fruit trees growing along the edge of an eighteen-acre pasture. There were many mango, lemon, orange, and banana trees. In addition, there were about sixty-five coffee plants. Though the land appeared fairly flat, with a slight slope towards the back of the property. A beautiful river with a sandy beach ran along the boundary of the property for about 700 feet. I visualized many children and adults playing in the shallow, clear water.

I saw three dilapidated houses on the property that would need to be demolished. An older man, his wife and their children lived in one of the houses while serving as caretakers. Two of the houses were at the front entrance. They both needed to be leveled, while the third house was at the back of the property. It also needed to be removed. Once again, I looked out at all the flat land that could be used as pasture for a good breed of cows and even some horses. I began to envision children working with the animals while others played on swings, played football, baseball, and basketball. I also envisioned many adults cuddling and caring for those little ones. The land had many possibilities and began to look like a paradise. We stood with Javier thinking of all the new responsibilities that would come with owning a property such as this. To begin with, the caretaker and his family had no money to make a move, so I felt the ministry would need to help them.

Whoever is kind to the needy honors God.
(Proverbs 14:31 NIV)

We would need to construct a seven-foot block security wall around the perimeter of the land. It would also need razor wire running completely around the top for added security. As I looked down the quarter-mile path to the back part of the property, I also realized we would need to bring electricity from the front of the property to the back where we were thinking of building the house for the children. Then there were the fruit trees that needed pruning, trimming, shaping, and stripping. The pasture needed mowing and replanting.

I asked Javier about education for the children and discovered there was no good, thriving school district nearby. We would have to take the children into Escuintla, which meant an hour and a half of dangerous driving every day unless we provided schooling on the property.

I felt a bit overwhelmed with the new responsibilities. I saw the possibilities for the land, but thought, *We don't even have enough money to buy this land. We're about thirty thousand dollars short of paying for it.* The cost of the property would be a small portion of what it would take to build the homes, barn, fencing, pasture, a school building, church building, and much more. It was beyond anything we could think or hope for. We prayed and looked to God for help knowing within our hearts He would meet all our needs.

My God shall supply all your need according to His riches in glory by Christ Jesus. (Philippians 4:19)

After seeing and walking across the land, we knew God was opening a door of opportunity for our commitment. I saw it as a place in future years that would be a paradise for an abused child. Yet, I knew that the only way it was going to happen was with unwavering dependence on God. God would need to do it. It was beyond my capability.

Back at our hotel in the quietness of the night, we prayed and looked to God. The next morning, we talked to Javier and Mariela. We were certain God's hand was on the property in Brito. I remembered the day we stopped with Mike and Penny and prayed for God's help to provide property in that area to build homes for abused children to live and rebuild their lives.

The next day, we met with a Christian attorney to begin the process of putting together the legal documents to purchase the land. When the seller heard of our purpose for the land, he deducted $2,000 from the total price and gave us three months to raise the money.

When the initial legal documents were ready, the contract of intent to purchase the land was signed. We then returned to the states to raise the money. God's favor was with us. We never solicited one church, organization, or person for a donation. We only told the story of what God was doing through us.

For You, O Lord, will bless the righteous; with favor You will surround him as with a shield. (Psalm 5:12)

In Guatemala City, it took several weeks of going through all the legal steps to purchase the property. As each step was cleared and completed, we would see God supplying all we needed to make the purchase happen. He not only supplied more than enough finances, He did it in less time than we thought possible.

Several years prior to the thought of helping abused children, God spoke a word to me through my friend, Giovanni. I was walking alone on a street at the conference center in Guatemala when my friend walked toward me. I greeted him as we passed each other.

Suddenly, Giovanni stopped and said, "Hey Don, just a minute."

I turned around and walked back to him. Giovanni told me at that very moment God gave him a word for me: "If you press forward in every way and stay faithful to the call I have given you, you will never have a lack for any need to do My work."

We shook hands, I thanked Giovanni for being faithful to God's Word, and continued on my way. Since then, I have learned to lay all our needs at God's feet. I have never seen God unfaithful to His Word. God has supplied all the people, animals, finances, and other needs to fulfill the vision He gave us.

With God supplying all we needed in the states to purchase the land, we returned to Guatemala. When we arrived, we were told that the Guatemalan legal work was also completed for the land purchase and it was time to move forward. Joy was in our hearts as we met with the attorney, the seller, and Javier. Within less than an hour, all the paperwork was completed and we were on our way to Brito. We desired to walk on the land again knowing that soon many little children would be cared for there.

When we arrived at the property, we saw how the weeds had grown even taller than when we first saw the property, but the fruit trees didn't appear to need as much pruning as we first thought. The property looked so beautiful. I knew that God made this purchase possible.

I realized the first necessity was to get electricity to the back part of the property. The public electric company quoted $18,000 to do the work. Since it was an absolute necessity, I agreed to the price. I was also told that it would take about three months before the electric company could begin the work. This was a blessing since we didn't yet have the money to pay for it. Barb and I returned home to begin raising the money.

I took on building decks and painting houses to raise money. Bringing electric to the back part of the property and construction of the first house were our primary concerns. We could see the favor of God again upon our work. Donations came from England as well as the eastern and western parts of the United States. Within six months, enough money was raised to cover the initial cost of construction of the first house and getting electric service. I was confident God would continue to supply all we needed for building the first house plus building the security wall around the 26 ½ acres of land we now owned.

Directly after purchasing the land in Brito, a small lot became available ten minutes away from our Brito land. I felt it was inexpensive and would be good to purchase it for Pedro and his family to build a small house. Meeting with our attorney again, the small parcel of land was purchased and deeded to Pedro and his family. I also offered them all the concrete blocks and metal and any other material they could salvage from the demolition of the existing houses on the Brito property. Pedro and his wife were thrilled. For the first time in their lives, they were about to own their own home.

The demolition of the first house on the back corner of the property began. It only took a little more than a week to complete the demolition and clear all the rubble from the land. After Javier and I talked to several different builders, we chose one to build the first house. Within two weeks the work had begun.

The first house was built to accommodate twelve children and four house parents. Each time we found some free time from visiting pastors and their churches, we would drive out to Brito to see how the project was progressing. It was exciting for us to watch Guatemalan construction. There were concrete foundations poured under all exterior and interior walls. All the walls were built using concrete blocks.

Through wisdom a house is built, and by understanding it is established; by knowledge the rooms are filled with all precious and pleasant riches. (Proverbs 24:3-4)

There was a team of caring church people that came each year from England to help in the construction of the homes. Bob Hamer was the team leader and they all seemed to thoroughly enjoy working together. For several days, they carried concrete blocks from ground level to the second floor of the house. Hired help was used to construct the second story walls.

When Barb and I returned to Brito after being away for more than a month, we saw the construction of the house had taken shape and it looked beautiful. It appeared about two more months of work would be needed to finish it. During our time at Brito, I talked to the builder concerning the cost of building the security wall around the perimeter of the land. It was a huge cost to build this wall but was needed to provide a secure place for the children to live. I gave the contract to the builder and had men working on the wall by the beginning of the next week.

There were trees up and down the property line to contend with. The workers cut some of them out of the way and others were dug up to make way for the wall. There were huge trees that were too big to remove so they built the wall right up to them. It gave the appearance that the wall was going through the center of the tree. It took nearly four months to complete the wall. Razor wire was mounted on top of the wall and the wall became a great blessing for all who lived on the property.

With the construction of the first house and the security wall, I asked Javier and Mariela, and their young family to move into the new house. I felt Javier and Mariela would one day be leading this ministry. The young couple accepted the challenge and promptly made their new residence in Brito.

Our daughter-in-law, Monica brought a team of ladies from St. Louis to put the finishing touches on the newly constructed house and prepare it for the first children that would come to live there.

Seven incredible ladies completely painted every wall in every room of the house. Then they painted murals giving each room its own identity. There was the football room, the ship room, the clown room, the jungle room, the cupcake room, the girl's bow room, the banner bathroom, and the welcome entryway. There was also a tree with leaves on it painted on the walls in the living room and dining room. The supporting post at the outer edge of the living room was made to look like a vine with leaves. The two rooms for house parents had scriptures painted along the top edge of the walls.

I tell you the truth, whatever you did for one of the least of these brothers of mine, you did for me. (Matthew 25:40 NIV)

The team brought gifts for the children who would occupy these rooms. They wanted a child arriving for the first time to feel welcome. They went to a furniture store in Escuintla and purchased living room and bedroom furniture for each room of the house. They also purchased two single beds for each child's bedroom.

With everything ready for children to come and be cared for, I invited the Guatemalan pastoral team working with me to come and celebrate the goodness of God for the finished work. They came and prayed over the house and the land and praised God for His goodness and blessing our efforts. Phase one of building the first house and the security wall was complete. It was time for us to take a break.

New responsibilities came for us in Guatemala we knew nothing about and we would experience new faith in God through a closer and more intimate relationship with Him. I would also find more love from God to bring us through the new trials we had never walked through before. New challenges were on the horizon, but we knew without a doubt God was with us.

Chapter 15

VICTORS NOT VICTIMS

This is the victory that has overcome the world-our faith.
(1 John 5:4)

Javier and Mariela came to Brito feeling a little apprehensive about living in rural Guatemala. At the same time, they were excited to be part of a new work that God was raising up. They brought their two small children and their twins with them. Along with the six of them came Jorge, a sixteen-year-old boy Javier had taken under his wing.

Jorge was a diligent worker and helped in constructing a road which ended at the entrance to the garage of the newly built house. The road at the back of the property was needed since Javier and family were now living on site. The many needs surfacing reminded Barb and me of the depth of commitment this project was requiring from us.

It was late spring and the rainy season had just begun. Javier and family were beginning to enjoy the rural lifestyle. Then came the seasonal rains that didn't seem to quit. In the midst of their weariness from the rains, a flash flood hit Brito. It became obvious that destruction was on the way.

The entrance to the base of the front door of the new house was about six feet higher than the crest of the river during normal times. But now, the river was within one inch of flooding the new house with muddy water. Javier and family began carrying their furniture to the second floor thinking the muddy water was coming into the house. Not only the house was targeted by the raging river, but a portion of the security wall protecting the property from the river was completely destroyed. The flood seemed to be bent on devastating all the work on the twenty-six acres of land.

However, I knew what God had said when the enemy came in like a flood, it left faster than it entered.

We were excited knowing that God's grace was upon all of us. No one was harmed, the muddy river water never came into the house, and the new security wall could be replaced with a steel rail wall. The new wall would never again be destroyed by floodwater from a raging river because the wall would allow water to pass through.

The LORD will cause your enemies who rise against you to be defeated before your face; they shall come out against you one way and flee before you seven ways. (Deuteronomy 28:7)

Cleanup was completed in a short time and the on-going construction work on the property progressed. I saw all that Javier,

Mariela, and Jorge were doing and began praying for an answer to how we could help them.

Early one morning while we were at home in the states, God planted a thought in my heart. There was a young man in Guatemala, Daniel Gonzalez, who was fluent in Spanish and English. I knew Daniel quite well because he had done some translating for me. If Daniel could work full time for me, he could do all my translating plus the administrative work with the churches. He could also serve with Javier in Brito reducing some of Javier's workload. *How great this would be for all of us,* I thought.

After much prayer, we believed this was the direction that God was taking us, so I called Daniel that evening and offered him a position as a full-time translator and administrator to us in Guatemala. I asked Daniel to seek God to know that this opportunity was from God and not from us. I gave him two months to make a decision.

You will seek the Lord your God, and you will find Him if you seek Him with all your heart and with all your soul. (Deuteronomy 4:29)

After two months of silence, I received a call from Daniel saying he wanted the position. He desired to give his present employer one-month notice before leaving. I was excited about the new arrangement.

The work was expanding and we needed even more help. It was time for me to break away from all the administrative work to think and pray. We relaxed best by driving and talking about our lives, our ministry, and our family. Since I loved the western part of the United States, it wasn't long before we were in our car and traveling out West.

As I drove towards Rolla, Missouri, we both began singing and praising God. It was then that God began speaking to me about moving to Guatemala. I didn't know how to share this thought of moving to Guatemala with Barb, so I prayed silently for God's help to know when and what words to use. We continued to praise and worship God.

After passing through Springfield, Missouri, a peace came over our car and I knew it was the time to begin to share what was in my heart. Barb sat quietly as I began to speak what I believed God put on my heart. When I finished, I just sat quietly. Finally, I broke the silence by asking Barb what she thought about what I had shared with her.

She sat there for what seemed like forever to me and then finally spoke. She said she didn't know how to respond because she had heard nothing from God. I told her we both needed to hear from God. Barb agreed. It became quiet in the car. I prayed silently and promised God I would wait for Barb as long as it took for her to make such a huge decision.

Two weeks later, we were in California just leaving the Los Angeles area. I had been driving for many hours. The sun had set and darkness surrounded our vehicle. Barb took over driving to give me a break. She did well on that straight highway through the desert.

Early the next morning as we passed through Las Vegas, I took the wheel while Barb rested. Soon we both felt refreshed and were excited about heading back home. During the past two weeks, not one word had been spoken of the possibility of fulltime work for the two of us in Guatemala. As we prayed, sang, and talked about the future, I felt the time was right to ask Barb if she had heard anything from God about working fulltime in Guatemala.

She thought for a while and then told me she had been praying, but still had not received any definite direction from God. She then said she knew she was ready to follow God and do whatever God was leading me to do. I rejoiced in hearing this because I knew it was God who had spoken to me nearly two weeks ago concerning fulltime work in Guatemala. I desired to care for the pastors as a father figure would care for sons. Excitement began to grow in both of us. After returning home from our vacation, we made plans for a trip to Guatemala. We desired to be living in Guatemala by the beginning of the New Year. We would need to share our new direction of living in Guatemala with our family, the brothers on the team, and their wives. We also needed to find a fully furnished apartment to rent in Guatemala. Our travel plans were coming together and excitement was filling our hearts.

Towards the end of the year, we traveled to Guatemala to put together our living arrangements. We met with our team, looked at apartments, and met with the sales manager at the hotel where we were staying. The best option God showed us was to continue to live at that hotel. We were given a suite on the eleventh floor. A fair price was offered and we accepted. God had put all the pieces of the great puzzle together and in the first few days of the new year, we moved to Guatemala to give personal spiritual covering to the pastors.

Living in Guatemala

I immediately began working closely with the pastors of the seventeen churches I was spiritually covering. I also spoke with Javier and Mariela to work more closely with the government to get legal status for the work of caring for abused children.

Month after month, we failed to receive legal status for having an orphanage on our property. Javier told us how the office of serving orphan children was constantly making new demands and changes to their rules and regulations. First, they were told a medical clinic needed to be built, then a school building, then more secure walls, then the river was too dangerous. It never ended. We became more and more frustrated as time passed. Three years passed and there still weren't any abused children living in the house that was built to house twelve children.

We kept meeting with the pastors and their wives while preaching nightly. Daniel worked with me translating each night in different churches. Barb felt that Raquel, Daniel's wife, would be a great asset to the work in Brito, but I didn't want to pay another monthly salary. Barb continued reasoning with me why Raquel would be an important helpmate in the ministry. I continued to pray to know God's will. I finally agreed.

Javier petitioned me to hire some men to work on the property. We selected four men and gave them a donation each month according to how many days they worked. After a few months of using donations to pay these four hired men, one of the men told the others they weren't receiving full employee benefits. Looking at all that was happening, we sought legal advice from an attorney. He told us what we were doing was legal, but if an employee ever challenged us in the courts, we would lose the case. We then met with another attorney who recommended we do all things strictly according to the law.

We began to pray to know God's will on how to hire people to work for our ministry. Questions came to my heart that helped clarify our decision. "What would you expect from someone if they came to our country to build a ministry? Would you want them to deal totally legally in every way with those serving you or try to get out of paying your employees what the government says you need to pay them?" The answer was obvious. We would want to do everything legal though it would cost us a lot more money. I would tell all those working for us in Brito they would receive all the benefits the government said they needed to receive. When my decision was made and announced, a new peace came over me that went beyond all understanding.

> *Be anxious for nothing, but in everything by prayer and supplication, with thanksgiving, let your requests be made known to God; and the peace of God, which surpasses all understanding, will guard your hearts and minds through Christ Jesus.* (Philippians 4:6)

We had been living in Guatemala for about two months when I remembered the vision I had received from the movie about two women helping abused children in the United States. I remembered the big red barn with a white rail fence. To make this happen in Brito, we would need to return to the States to find the material to build a big red animal barn. Returning home, we found a company in Oklahoma that manufactured metal buildings. We drove there and found the exact type of building we wanted. We also found a manufacturer of white vinyl fencing. We placed an order for the material for the barn and the fencing to be shipped to our warehouse in Wentzville, Missouri. It was then loaded on two forty-foot containers and shipped to Guatemala. When the two containers arrived at the property in Brito, they knocked the top of the entranceway down entering the property since it was too low for the containers to pass under. Another challenge was finding someone to build the barn. I was informed that no one in Guatemala had ever built this kind of building, but by the grace of God, Daniel and I located a builder who agreed to do the construction work when all was ready in Brito.

The next hurdle was to purchase a farm tractor. After many days of searching, Daniel and I found one with the implements we felt we needed. The tractor enabled us to do the work around the farm.

Our new association was then formed entitled, "Niños Amados," meaning "Loving Children." Barb, three of our sons, and I served as officers of the board, and Daniel Gonzalez became the legal representative of our newly formed association. Raquel began working with CNA to obtain legal authorization to have an orphanage in Brito, Guatemala.

CNA is the government entity that has legal oversight over orphanages, orphans, and needy children in Guatemala.

During the day, Barb and I continued to meet with pastors and their wives. Five nights each week, I kept my preaching alive by sharing messages in the churches. After the message each night, I would have a time of ministry with God's people. This ministry time would last from thirty minutes to an hour. Often several people would give their lives to Jesus. It was a great time for me as I took pleasure in bringing truth to God's people. Barb was always at my side supporting me in every decision I made.

If you abide in Me, and My words abide in you, you will ask what you desire, and it shall be done for you. (John 15:7)

Our Days in Court

One day while Javier was in Guatemala City running errands, two men walked on the property and talked to Mariela. They told her they were the owners of the land. They said Mariela and Javier and their family were living on the land illegally and they would need to vacate immediately. They also told Mariela that for many thousands of dollars Mariela and Javier could pay them and they would turn over all rights to the property.

That night when Javier returned from the city, Mariela told him about the two men who entered the property that day and told her that she and her family needed to leave the property. Javier told me what transpired and therefore we were advised to seek legal counsel. Such discussions happened several times and I became concerned for the progress of building the work for abused children.

About six months later, I was scheduled to meet with our team at 6:30 p.m. at the hotel. Barb and I were leaving in the morning to return home for three days. On this particular Monday afternoon, I was down in the lobby paying my bill and thinking about the two men who had come on the property several times saying they were the owners of the land. While I was walking to the elevators to return to my room, a little voice spoke to my inner being and said, "Call Carlos Lopez!" He was an attorney we had recently met. I didn't know if we could trust him, so I thought, *No, I'm not calling him.*

As I stepped into the elevator, the voice spoke again saying, "Call Carlos Lopez!"

Again I thought, *No, I'm not calling this man.* Entering our room, I told Barb what had just happened and asked her what she thought I should do. Barb said I needed to obey the voice that was speaking to me. So, I called Carlos and told him what had transpired. Carlos asked to meet with me immediately. I told him to come to the hotel by 5:00 p.m. and I would have one hour to talk with him before my team meeting began.

It was 6:15 when Carlos finally found me in the lobby. Carlos had been there for more than an hour looking for me while I had been looking for him. I told him it was too late to meet, but Carlos asked for just fifteen minutes. I reluctantly agreed and we went to a private area in the lobby. I did my best to quickly explain all that had recently happened.

Carlos then asked me for permission to go to the courts in the morning to see if there were any cases filed against our association.

I told him, "No, it's all too confusing to make an important decision this quickly."

Carlos shared with me that there could be a danger for our work in Guatemala if these men were trying to falsely make claims to this land. Being pressed for time and not knowing Carlos Lopez very well, I decided to leave well enough alone.

I met with the team, helped Barb finish packing, and slept a few hours before boarding our flight home the next morning. We arrived home at 3:30 p.m. that afternoon and looked forward to a full night's rest in our own bed, but God had another plan for me.

Around 6:30 that evening, Carlos called me from Guatemala. He informed me that though I did not give him permission to go to the courts, he went anyway. He only wanted to find out if there were any cases on the books against our association owning the land. He found that there was a big problem filed against our association. Over two months ago, our Guatemalan association was supposedly legally notified of an allegation against it and said we had nine days to reply. Since we were never informed of this notification, we never responded and the nine days had passed. We were now in contempt of court. A hearing was requested by the plaintiffs to evict our association from our property.

A problem arose and the court didn't get the hearing scheduled. No judgment was filed against our association nor any eviction notice given. I had no idea any of this was happening. Carlos asked me to give him the authority to continue to watch for anything new from the courts. I told Carlos we would be returning on Friday, but Carlos was adamant that by the following Monday it could be too late to correct the situation. I asked Carlos what it would cost to have him do this work for us. He told me he would contact his team of lawyers, get their advice, and call back with more specifics.

About two hours later, Carlos called giving me three different options of payment for this type of case making its way through the courts. The cost was enormous. Barb and I couldn't believe what was happening. I told Carlos I would need to pray to know God's will in this matter.

Call upon Me in the day of trouble; I will deliver you, and you shall glorify Me. (Psalm 50:15)

As we prayed for God's wisdom to come down from heaven, He answered our prayer by giving me an idea. I didn't want to take a chance of giving Carlos a large sum of money and never see him again. I believed this would never happen, but at this moment I knew I needed to move forward slowly until I had a good relationship built with Carlos.

My agreement with Carlos was to pay him one-fourth of the total amount up front and then another fourth in six months if the case went that long. I would then pay another fourth in one year. The last fourth would be paid when the case ended. Carlos and his team agreed and it wasn't long before a lawsuit had begun. For the next year and a half, we prayed continuously for victory. Our association won our case in each court we passed through because God was with us from the beginning. The property was victoriously won for the needy and abused children of Guatemala. I hired a guard for the front gate allowing no one to enter the property without prior authorization. We had put the entire lawsuit in God's hands, convinced He was in control of all the courts and our proceedings. When the fear of losing the land and the work for children overtook me, I would not accept it.

> **I knew fear comes from the enemy and had already been bound in heaven, so I bound it here on Earth. The victory was the Lord's!**

We knew there was much more on the horizon for us. Though we knew there would still be challenges, we spoke a quote we had heard Joel Osteen declare: "We are the victors, not the victims."

Chapter 16

AN INESCAPABLE CRASH

He changes times and seasons; he sets up kings and deposes them. He gives wisdom to the wise and knowledge to the discerning. (Daniel 2:21)

Change is inevitable. The original staff and maintenance crew left for the lack of orphans to care for. Little by little a new staff came and began to work diligently to obtain legal status for the orphanage in Brito. Daniel, continued on as administrator for the ministry and Raquel continued to work with C.N.A. to obtain legal status for the orphanage.

The work Raquel endured with C.N.A. was a long, time-consuming process. It took more than nine months of daily answering questions and filling out forms before our association received approval to have the orphanage in Guatemala. With the paperwork completed, all documentation was kept in book form under Raquel's care. The hand of God was over Daniel and Raquel working with all the paperwork to achieve victory. At the beginning of the New Year, a celebration was declared when the news came that the legal document was granted. Once the orphanage was declared legal, the children began to arrive.

The first orphan child that came to Brito was an infant no more than a couple weeks old. She was abandoned and found on the streets of a small community in Guatemala. Taken to the courts, she was given the name, "Estrella De Jesus" which means "Star of Jesus." She was the first of many that came to Brito. Within ten months, there were twenty-five orphans living in the first home that was built to accommodate twelve children. It was agreed by the directors at that time that there were too many children in the home and the number needed to be reduced to no more than eighteen children.

With a new staff and new maintenance crew working on the property, construction of the barn and the white fence began. Six months after beginning the barn construction project, it was completed. It looked beautiful and was strongly constructed.

Along with building the barn, the pasture needed renovation. It was 10 percent grass and 90 percent weeds. Daniel and I visited several companies that gave us advice on how to prepare the soil and the type of grass seed to sow. We wanted to grow the best pasture we could for large animals. In less than a month, we began seeing a green pasture popping up from the dark brown soil.

Dogs and cats were also part of the vision. We purchased two golden retriever puppies. The children enjoy these two playful dogs. One is named Barkleigh and the other is Cosmos. The name Barkleigh honored Sally and Gwen from Pennsylvania who helped us raise many donations for construction projects at the orphanage. Cosmos was named in honor of our sons' company that was faithful to the project of serving the poor in various nations around the world.

The river that runs along one side of the Brito property was perfect for children and adults to enjoy. During the non-rainy season, it is only four feet deep in its deepest part and the water is crystal clear. The children also enjoy swimming and playing in areas of the sand beach.

We stayed busy with the Brito project. At the same time, churches came to us seeking spiritual covering. When we were not in Brito, we were visiting pastors and their wives to pray with them and learn their needs. The ministry began to blossom because of the interest we took in the families of the pastors we worked with. These families sensed the presence of God in all we undertook.

If a man does not know how to rule his own house, how will he take care of the church of God? (1 Timothy 3:5)

Gratia Institute

Darin, our second eldest son, came to Guatemala for a third time to preach among the churches with me. At the end of Darin's two weeks in Guatemala, he commented how it appeared the work was growing and doing well. He also added that an institute to train future leaders for the churches in Guatemala was needed.

I knew Darin was right. I also knew I didn't have the time to devote to raising up another new ministry for teaching pastors and leaders. We began to pray, seeking God's direction for a discipleship-training institute in Guatemala.

We all flew home together. While at home one morning, I met Darin for breakfast and asked Darin to pray about helping us in forming an institute to train men and women for Christian service in the Kingdom of God in Guatemala.

Darin responded immediately, "I have been praying about it for a long time. God has already spoken to me. I know it's right and I want to do this with you and mom."

My head was spinning. I was so full of joy in what I was hearing. I had no idea this would be Darin's response. I was overjoyed! It didn't take long for Darin to be on a flight to Guatemala. Upon arriving, he and I began looking for a location to build or purchase a building to house about twelve students each year. The plan was for students to be in class five days a week for nine months of the year. We reviewed many properties but found only one location that Darin liked. It was a small plot of land high on the side of a mountain. Someone had built the foundation of a large home, but never finished it. It looked a mess to me, but Darin thought it was great.

I discovered I knew the owner, Jose Miguel. He was a pastor of one of our churches. He had talked to me, in the past, about purchasing this property from him, but I hadn't been interested in it.

Later in the year, I was with him in Miami. While we were riding through the city, a text came in on his cellular. It stated that he and his family had received their residency approval to live and work in the United States for as long as they wanted. Jose Miguel handed the phone to me to read. I was excited for him and his family.

Jose Miguel's visa would have terminated in August without renewal. It was June when he received their residency approval.

With this victory, he asked me if I wanted the house in Guatemala. I told him Darin was very interested in it. He told me he would sell it to us at a ridiculously low price. He said that he told God he would do this if God would give him his residency. I accepted Jose Miguel's kindness, preached on Sunday, and returned home the next day. Darin excitedly accepted the building for training young people to do God's work.

I was walking on air, thanking God for His provision once again!

He. . .gave some to be pastors and teachers, to prepare God's people for works of service. (Ephesians 4:12)

When we returned to Guatemala, Darin and I interviewed several builders to rebuild the house by adding more bedrooms and completely changing the floor plan to make it work for the institute. The finished product turned out to be a great blessing for all who were involved with it.

Darin gave the name "Gratia" to the institute and all its teachings. During the last half of the year, he began interviewing young people to be students in a class that would begin in the middle of the first month of the New Year. By the end of the year, Darin had eleven students ready to begin their studies in Gratia.

After two weeks of much preparation, Darin returned home to the states while we remained in Guatemala. I kept extremely busy with the monthly pastoral retreats, preparing teachings for the

Gratia Institute, preaching in the churches, and leading the team at its' meetings.

Our heads were spinning as we saw ourselves working in many directions in the ministry. Among all the activities mentioned, there was added new construction on a second house for Brito. It was beginning to get underway. There was also new construction beginning on a new house for the directors of the orphanage, Daniel and Raquel. In addition to the construction projects, there was the purchase of a horse and a gift of a second one for the children to enjoy. One young girl living on the property said she was experienced in caring for horses. I asked her to take responsibility for protecting the smaller children around the horses and caring for the horses. She agreed, but after a short time, she left Brito to return to her mother's home.

Do not worry about tomorrow, for tomorrow will worry about itself. Each day has enough trouble of its own. (Matthew 6:34 NIV)

The Dreams

We once again felt overwhelmed with our workload. We just kept pressing on. Then, in the middle of the night in the spring of 2012, I had a dream. I saw myself driving a large tractor-trailer on a four-lane highway coming out of St. Louis. I was driving the truck about sixty miles per hour going around a long, sharp curve. At the last minute, I saw an automobile stopped in front of me on the highway. I knew there was no way to prevent a terrible accident.

I remembered seeing children in the car. I saw myself standing on the brakes, but it was impossible to stop that massive rig. The trailer began sliding sideways down the highway until it was right alongside me. The truck was completely out of control. I knew if I hit the car it would be demolished and possibly kill someone. I screamed at the top of my lungs. I jumped up and continued to scream.

By that time, Barb was awake and hollering at me to settle down. I was crying as I told her about the dream. I kept saying I didn't understand why I was having this terrible dream. I told her it was so real, I felt it was really happening. I continued to cry as Barb and I laid back down and began to pray. We asked God what this dream meant.

At that moment, God began to speak to me and said, "If you don't slow down, you're going to crash."

I immediately asked God to forgive me and promised I would slow down my busy lifestyle.

Be still and know that I am God. (Psalm 46:10)

The next morning as we left our hotel room, I felt everyone was staring at me. They really weren't, but I thought I possibly woke everyone in the hotel at 2:00 a.m. the night before with my screaming.

Many months passed and I eventually forgot about the dream. I also forgot my promise to God. We were in our usual routine of busyness. We had retreats to contend with, I was still preaching many nights each week, and leading the team meetings every Monday night. The second children's house was nearing completion along with the director's house.

In October of 2012, I had another dream. The second dream also took place in the middle of the night at the same hotel in Guatemala City. In my dream I was driving on the same highway as before coming out of St. Louis, but this time I was driving a loaded dump truck too fast. I was coming around a long, sharp curve in the highway and saw a car at a dead stop on the highway. Again, I wasn't able to stop the huge, heavy dump truck. I saw that the dump truck was going to go right over the top of the car and that everyone in that car would be killed.

I woke up screaming and shaking. My loud screaming woke Barb. I was crying while trying to tell Barb about the dream and how similar it was to the first dream months ago. We began to pray, but I knew what this dream meant without asking God for its meaning. I began repenting before the Lord, asking God to forgive me again. This time I promised I would definitely slow down.

> *You do not delight in sacrifice, or I would bring it; you do not take pleasure in burnt offerings. The sacrifices of God are a broken spirit; a broken and contrite heart, O God, you will not despise.* (Psalm 51:16-17) *NIV*

From then until the end of November, I tried to slow down since things were going fairly well. Then I began taking on a little more each week until by the end of the year, I was back to my usual busyness. Throughout the first half of the New Year, we were working continuously in Guatemala.

On one specific trip, we traveled high into mountainous regions visiting churches over an eight-day period. Two days before we were to return to Guatemala City, the seasonal rains began, and as usual, there seemed to be no end to them. After two days of continuous rain, the highways were experiencing many mudslides.

We were staying in Quezaltenango high in the mountains at a retreat center. The news came that the mountainous highway we would be driving in the morning was closed because of mudslides covering the highway in several locations. It was reported it would be shut down for several days. This meant we would miss our next commitments in Guatemala City.

In the morning, I was told that another road through the mountains was open for travel and was passable. However, it was a back road, not a highway and some of the roads would be dirt or mud. I had confidence in the brother that brought me the news and trusted him to give me good advice. So, on Saturday morning Pablo, Barb and I with an Indian lady who needed to get to Guatemala City, began our travel into regions of Guatemala we had never visited before.

Pablo kept me on the right road by getting directions from various people in the villages and small towns we traveled through. For the first four hours, things went well. Then, high on the side of a mountain on a mud road, there was a long line of vehicles waiting to cross a rickety wood and iron bridge. The gorge under the bridge was hundreds of feet straight down. I sat in line behind a yellow bus that was at the entry to the bridge. There were trucks, buses, and cars behind me waiting to cross, but the yellow bus wouldn't move. I drove alongside it and inquired if the bridge was safe to drive across. The bus driver said he didn't know. We all began to pray asking God if it was safe to cross the bridge.

> *Have no fear of sudden disaster or of the ruin that overtakes the wicked, for the LORD will be your confidence and will keep your foot from being snared.* (Proverbs 3:25 NIV)

I began to slowly cross the rickety old bridge, creeping along so as to not make any vibration on the bridge. We were praying all the way to the other side. When we made it to the opposite side, everyone gave thanks to God for safe travel. We finally arrived at the hotel in Guatemala City early that evening. We all rejoiced in the Lord for giving us safe passage.

The Crash

Barb and I returned to the States to take a vacation in the Dominican Republic at a beautiful resort. We were both looking forward to our time away from work. When the day came to start our vacation, we boarded our flight with much joy and excitement. We just wanted to lie on the beach, soak up the sun, and read a book or two. While away, we spent time talking about the past year and all the growth we'd seen in the ministry. The new construction of house #2 had been completed along with the house for Daniel and Raquel. Another area of growth was in the churches. New pastors were coming to the one-day retreats and receiving much knowledge and revelation from those who were teaching during these wonderful times.

Every day before breakfast, we would do our individual physical exercises. I had just about finished mine and was on the last bit of the workout. My final exercise was to stand up straight and bend forward to touch the floor with my fingertips. As I bent over to touch the floor, I felt a sharp pain in my back. Down I went, flat on my face in excruciating pain. It was the worst experience of my life.

For more than twenty-four hours, I laid on a couch in one position and could only crawl to the bathroom. By midnight, Barb went looking for a doctor hoping to relieve my pain. Finding one in the hotel, she brought him to our room. After examining me, the doctor said that he could give me injections in my back to temporarily get rid of some of the pain.

If you suffer for doing good and you endure it, this is commendable before God. (1 Peter 2:20 NIV)

Ten minutes after receiving three injections, the pain began to subside. I was able to stand up and walk to the bed. Barb got our flight changed to return home the next morning. The doctor recommended I come to his hotel office in the morning for three more injections. The next morning at 6:30 a.m., I went in a wheelchair to the doctor's office to receive three more painful injections in my back. By 9:00 a.m., we were on our way to the airport. The airline furnished me with a wheelchair to go from the shuttle to the check-in desk.

At the check-in desk, we were informed our flight had been canceled and we would leave the next morning. Sitting in the wheelchair, I explained to the agent at the counter what had transpired over the last thirty hours and that the injections I received at the hotel would only give me about twelve hours of relief. I then asked the attendant in a gracious manner to get us on another airline.

After about an hour of diligently trying to help us, the flight attendant was finally able to get us booked on a different airline that was scheduled to leave in two hours. We were thankful to the airline, but mostly to God for making a flight available to us.

When the flight arrived in Miami, Barb was put in one wheelchair and I in another. The attendants did this to move us more quickly through the airport. There were thousands of people waiting to get through immigration and customs. Since we were each in wheelchairs, our drivers seemed to zip right through the long lines of people.

When we arrived home, Barb took me right to a pain specialist. He administered three more painful injections. I then contacted a bone specialist to see if he could repair whatever happened in my back. After a series of tests, I was informed I had a broken disk. The doctor set me up to have microscopic back surgery the next day. After the surgery, I felt like a new man. I walked long distances with no pain and felt highly blessed for the goodness of God in my life.

> *Those who wait on the Lord will gain new strength.*
> (Isaiah 40:31)

I acknowledged I caused this crash in my life by my refusal to do as God had instructed and slow down. I have always found it very difficult to slow down my activities in the ministry, but I committed in my heart to obey the will of God. I had learned a "crash" is much more painful than doing what God asks us to do.

Jehovah Forever

In late summer, Barb and I traveled to Guatemala to visit the orphanage and some of the churches. We also met with Mike Stevens who had come to Guatemala to preach in the churches and teach in Gratia Institute for several days.

One morning after breakfast with Mike, we shared with him what had transpired over the past twenty-four months. Mostly we shared concerning the lawsuit against the property in Brito. Mike suggested we all go and pray over the property. When we arrived in Brito, Mike was greatly encouraged by what he saw. There were now nearly fifty children and many adults living there. Mike suggested we walk across the property praying in the Spirit of our God.

The sky was blue and clear on a beautiful windless day as about twelve people joined us on our prayer-walk. Mike prayed loudly with all his heart for several minutes. Barb and I were walking hand-in-hand as usual. When Mike stopped praying, I began to pray forcibly, angry with the enemy. I knew the enemy was trying to steal the property from our association again using the courts to move against us.

I cried out loudly with all my heart and with all the volume of my voice, "AND YOUR NAME JEHOVAH WILL BE WRITTEN IN STONE ON THIS LAND FOREVER."

Just as the word "forever" left my lips, a crack of thunder that sounded like a shotgun being fired directly next to our ears, confirmed God's name would be written on stone in this land forever. With this declaration, I was prophetically declaring that the land belonged to God and no one would ever steal it from Him. God had thundered, "YES."

I worked with Daniel for several months to get this inscription written on the huge stone by the front gate for all to see as they entered the property. Within a week of the inscription being completed in marble mounted on the large stone, I received a call from the attorney stating our case was won in the Supreme Court. **The lawsuit was over!** Our association had won its case in the highest court in the land.

> *My word that goes out from my mouth: It will not return to me empty, but will accomplish what I desire and achieve the purpose for which I sent it.* (Isaiah 55:11) *NIV*

Rejoicing in the Lord over all that God had done in Brito, the churches and the institute were viewed by us as miracles from heaven. Each miracle brought the knowledge of God's presence into our life as well as to the many others working with us.

We continued to oversee the work in Brito and the churches for another eighteen months. During this time, another builder was hired to construct house #3. It took nearly a year to build because of its size and the commercial kitchen that was built adjacent to it.

During this time Daniel and I purchased four registered, pregnant Hereford cows. Those four cows have now multiplied to bring their number to fourteen. Each of the cows and bulls is registered, branded, and carry a quality value to their presence on the land.

In addition to building a third house and purchasing four pregnant cows, several teams came to Brito. Different teams brought different furnishing for the houses. Bedding, curtains, decorative pictures for the walls and scores of other items were made available for the work in Brito. They brought toys, shoes, and clothing for the children. These handmade and store purchased items brought new life to the children and adults who came to occupy the new surroundings. Many blessings have come to us through these team members. We also know the blessings our sons and daughters have played in various parts of the ministry.

Our Legacy

As for me and my household, we will serve the LORD. (Joshua 24:15 NIV)

The first breakthrough into the mission field for us had come in February of 1988. Our youngest daughter, Darlene and I signed up to go on a short-term mission team to Guatemala. On that trip, we worked together constructing a new roof on a portion of a new building that would soon house many orphan children. Now, many years later, our eldest son, Don Jr., came to our home to talk to us about how he could help in the ministry. Knowing Don Jr's. love for children, I asked him to consider helping with the orphanage. I told our son that there was so much to do and we would count it a blessing if he would help in that area. Much conversation ensued after which Don Jr. went home and began to pray about all that was spoken that evening.

A few weeks later, Don Jr. met with us again and told us he wanted to be a part of the ministry to help abused children in Brito, Guatemala. We were excited to hear his decision. Don Jr. and his wife, Beth gave new leadership to the work in Brito. They brought about a beautiful and harmonious work for the abused children there. They took the living conditions of these children in Brito to a new level. Don Jr. organized the construction of a church and a school building while working closely with me in all major decisions. Beth helped young girls and women learn how to live out their lives for the glory of God. They have taken nearly all the work and responsibility off Barb and myself, which has given us a freedom we had not known for many years.

Darin has taken the work of Gratia Leadership Institute completely on his shoulders, and little by little has taken over the work of giving spiritual covering to the pastors that make up our team. We have seen Darin grow into an amazing man who carries a strong faith in God believing God is leading him in all his decisions.

Darin's wife Monica has worked from the beginning in bringing teams to Brito. She is an amazing woman who has a beautiful gift of putting into action what she envisions for the children. The paintings, murals, and pictures coordinate with the colors of each room and give a professional touch to make the homes a beautiful place for abused children to come, live, and get their lives in order.

Derrik continues to be a blessing in Haiti. He works in unity with another ministry that is feeding and caring for more than 750 children daily. He has also served and supported Strong Tower Ranch, which gives opportunities to under-privileged children from the inner city.

Our youngest son, Denver continues to be a support to the work in prayer, finances and caring for all technology with our computers functioning properly. He also promotes financial support working with Down syndrome children and an organization known as Options for Women. He and his family help us continue doing God's work in several nations around the world.

Anyone who has faith in me will do what I have been doing. He will do even greater things than these, because I am going to the Father. (John 14:12 NIV)

Our eldest daughter, Carol has a gift of sewing all types of bedding, curtains, pillow coverings, and much more. When guests come to walk through the homes for abused children, they not only see the beautiful interior designs on the walls but are taken in by the beautiful bedspreads, curtains, and pillow coverings inside the houses.

The projects throughout the history of this ministry have prospered and continue to meet the physical and spiritual needs of many. However, the challenges never end. We know the enemy will continue to try to stop God's work. I felt the enemy's persecution when cancer was brought upon our son, when he enabled the lawsuit against the work in Brito, and when he caused the accident in southern Mexico, plus numerous other trials and tribulations. However, the Lord delivered us from them all.

"Team of women who came with Monica to paint murals on the new home in Brito."

"Team of men pouring a concrete driveway in front of the 3 homes at the Brito orphanage."

"Red barn purchased in the United States and sent on a container to be constructed on the property in Brito."

"White fencing purchased in the states and sent on a container along with the red barn to Brito, Guatemala."

"After the renovation of the pasture, 4 pure bred pregnant Hereford cows were purchased because this quality of cows can be used for therapy to the hurting child."

An Inescapable Crash

"These are the two Golden Retrievers bringing enjoyment to the children."

"The children are now able to play in secure surroundings."

"School building construction completed in 2018, for grades K through 12."

"The children at the school have their own uniforms and are able to walk to the school in total security."

"This stone is placed at the front of the property and is one of the first things seen upon visitors entering." The English translation is:
"My name Jehovah will be written in stone on this property forever."

"Barb and I in Brito in April, 2018 and privileged to have our photo taken with all the children."

"Graduating class at Gratia Leadership Training Program in the Spring of 2017. Several of the teachers are on the front row."

"Gratia Leadership Institute with 2018 students."

Epilogue
"Barb's Keepsakes"

On December 26, 1990, with help from family and friends, Barb and I moved out of our home in Chesterfield, Missouri. All our personal belongings were boxed, and our furniture, tools, and appliances were put in a rented storage building. At the end of the day, we were in that large, empty house alone. All those who came early that morning to help had left. The day of moving was complete.

Coming in from outside I couldn't find Barb. I called out, "Barb, where are you?" I then heard a little muttering from, what used to be the master bedroom. As I entered I saw Barb sitting on that big, empty, carpeted, floor sobbing. She had all her little keepsakes on the floor around her. That's all she had left from all those years of serving God with me. Everything else was packed away and put in storage. She no longer had a home for her family to visit. I just sat down on the floor with her and held her tight.

"Everyone who has left houses or brothers or sisters or father or mother or children or fields for my sake will

receive a hundred times as much and will inherit eternal life." **(Matthew 19:29)**

Each of us has a life-story to tell. Our story has been to speak of God's faithfulness. So, we speak of His love to protect us, His kindness to prosper us, His joy to encourage us, and His peace to bring us through the storms of life. Through all this, He brings each of us to His eternal purpose for He knows the end from the beginning.

When the day of moving came to a close, we had nothing of material value left. Our sons and daughters went home when the work was finished. Our friends had all left after the last truck was loaded and taken to the small warehouse. There, we felt alone with no purpose in life to accomplish.

The next day Barb and I began our long journey through Mexico on our way to Guatemala to study Spanish. God had a purpose for our life. Though we couldn't see it, it was unfolding with each breath we took. Now, twenty-eight years later, as we look back through the span of time, we see what great manner of life God has led us through. We had no idea God would use us the way He has. His victories were innumerable though we didn't see them in their moments of time.

Each son and daughter of the King has an important life to enjoy in His presence. His Glory will shine forth bringing His purpose through the life He has given each of us.

I ask God frequently, "Why us Lord? Why have You blessed us so much?" The answer simply comes: "Because He loves us just as He does all His sons and daughters." We, as with all His family, are the apple of His eye. He will continue to take us forward and use us as long as we continue to respond to His calling and go.

After the packing of all our earthly belongings, we felt alone and broke. Then the knowledge of His grace and inner peace came and overwhelmed us. We now are receiving the inheritance He has for each of us.

Are you receiving your inheritance or are you living for the little keepsakes of life? God will show you as you continue to say yes to His calling. Your life will change, and you will do that which you never thought possible. Will you go for it? Each activity you take part in will grow into the impossible inheritance you never thought possible.

Donald D. Kassebaum

Contact information:
E-mail address is dbkassebaum@mac.com.
Barb's e-mail address is barbarakassebaum@me.com.
Our website is www.giftsofloveintl.com

CPSIA information can be obtained
at www.ICGtesting.com
Printed in the USA
FFHW020504161118
49444389-53774FF